treasures
in the darkness

a true story of life and love

andy bray

with jayna richardson

FAMILYLIFE®

LITTLE ROCK, ARKANSAS, USA

treasures in the darkness: a true story of life and love

Published by FamilyLife, 5800 Ranch Drive, Little Rock, Arkansas, 72223, U.S.A.
A ministry of Campus Crusade for Christ Inc.

Printed in New Zealand

ISBN: 978-1-60200-116-9

13 12 11 10 09 08   1 2 3 4 5 6 7

Authors: Andy Bray with Jayna Richardson
Editor: Jayna Richardson
Proofreaders: Fran Taylor and Jonathan Taylor
Graphic Designer: Jennifer I. Smith
Cover Photography: Creative Shotz

FAMILYLIFE NZ
Phone: 0800 800 680
email: info@familylife.org.nz
website: www.familylife.org.nz

To my amazing, beloved wife, Nikki.

Thank you for choosing to be my partner for life. Thank you for your constant sacrificial dedication through everything. Most of all, thank you for loving me even when I was at my most unlovable, and believing in me in even the darkest moments. You make every challenge, and my life, worthwhile. You are the best decision I ever made.

To Olivia and Benjamin.

You were uppermost in my mind as this book came together. This book is for each of you as I wanted to pass on some of the lessons I've learned. My prayer is that you will read this and grasp the significance of two vital things:

(1) That God is an integral part of the abundant, purpose-driven life. Make sure you maintain a personal relationship with Christ that is authentic and real, and

(2) The person you choose to marry is the second most important decision you will ever make. Choose wisely. Thank you for the joy, laughter, and meaning you have given me through the quality of your lives, and the many wonderful ways you express your love to me.

To Natasha.

You asked if you could read the manuscript (at your young age, you seemed so understanding of my challenges), but I said, "Wait for the printed book to come out." I regret that now. I hope you get to read it in heaven somehow. I look forward to asking you what you think of it. I miss you so much it aches, and my life seems incomplete without you. Thank you for the many rich memories and all the love you bestowed upon me. I am blessed and inspired by your short, power-filled life. Your life was a gift. I praise the sovereign God of the universe for all that you were to me and to so many others.

"And I will give you

treasures hidden in the darkness—

secret riches.

I will do this so you may

*know that I am the L*ORD*,*

the God of Israel, the one

who calls you by name."

—Isaiah 45:3 (NLT)

contents

photos follow page 82

foreword

When I first met Andy Bray over a decade ago, I was profoundly impressed with his heart for God and his desire to see New Zealand's families strengthened, one home at a time. To be honest, I'd never encountered a man quite like him. I doubt that you will either. You are about to encounter a great story of repentance, redemption, and resolve. This is no ordinary man that you are about to encounter. No, you are about to rub shoulders with a real man who will challenge you in the trials you face and the way you respond in faith.

It has been said that some men owe the grandeur of their lives to their many difficulties. Andy and his wife, Nikki, indeed have a grand story to tell. Any one of the issues they've faced could have destroyed them, their marriage, and their family. Kidney failure, a kidney transplant, cancer, rejection of the kidney (years later), dialysis, an operation, a stroke, and the death of their eldest daughter Natasha ... they have walked in and through the valley of the shadow of death a number of times.

As I read these pages, I reflected upon Andy and Nikki and their lives. Several words and phrases came to mind:

Authentic—they are the real deal. On more than one occasion I've marveled as they have allowed others into the interior of their lives.

This book is an authentic story about one man's struggle with God.

Hero—both are among the most courageous people I know. If I were in a war (and I am), I'd want Andy and Nikki on the front lines with me (and they are). They aren't quitters. They are heroic leaders who are taking back territory that for too long has been claimed by the enemy.

A man and woman of faith—some people talk about faith; others, like this pair, live it. Here and now. Not just once, but repeatedly.

Overcomer—perseverance is the mark of true leadership. I've been amazed to watch this gritty pair of Christ followers stand firm and lead others while facing challenges that are beyond my imagination.

If you are looking for encouragement, if you are looking for perspective, if you are looking for comfort, come and meet my friends Andy and Nikki. Jump into their lives through the pages of this book and you'll get more than you bargained for. They are good friends that I am counting on as I continue to run my race. I am honoured that they asked me to write this foreword.

May God bless Andy and Nikki. God certainly has blessed New Zealand, the world, and me through them!

Dennis Rainey
President, FamilyLife

acknowledgments

For years, friends such as Kevin Taylor and Des Moss have said to me, "Andy, you must write a book." Personally, I could never understand why, as it appeared to me that the only significant thing I've ever done is hang on for dear life and just try to make the best of things. If I were to write a book, it would be to pass on some life lessons to my children, and for them to have something to remember me by after I die.

Then, one day, out of the blue, my friend Drew Coons of FamilyLife in the United States, who has done so much to help our ministry in New Zealand develop the way we wanted it to, offered the skills and expertise of his assistant and author Jayna Richardson, to make sure this book happened. He even paid for her to come to New Zealand and spend some quality time with Nikki and me, getting to know us, and recording our story as we "re-lived" it. From then on, Jayna devoted hours to the task of assembling our garbled words and stories into some kind of order and giving them life.

This book is the result of both Drew's commitment, and Jayna's hard work, commitment, perseverance, and superb writing skills. I'm indebted to both of you for making this possible.

It's actually wonderful to have this unique opportunity to acknowledge some people and express my appreciation to them for their contributions. The danger is that, because it's not possible to name everyone, I cause offence for neglecting someone. (I have not included people who rallied around us after Natasha's death. You are too numerous to mention here.)

First, I want to acknowledge Dennis Rainey, the president of FamilyLife. Of all the people I have known, he is the one person who has influenced me the most. Dennis, it was your vision, your passion, and your real message that persuaded me that I needed to invest my life in something meaningful. I'm constantly inspired by your leadership to live a life of excellence and to trust God for great things. What you have done for families around the world is extraordinary.

To Bob and Kathy Helvey, and David and Alison Munn. Thank you for your vision and leadership back in 1990 that enabled the first FamilyLife Conference to be held in New Zealand. It was easy to come behind you, with your encouragement and support, and carry on what you started. Many of the systems and tools you created are still used today.

To Nikki's mum, Deana. Our ministry would not have been possible without you. We so appreciate you arranging your diary on numerous occasions to care for our children whenever we had to be away at a conference or seminar.

To Biffy Savage, thank you for your selfless support of Nikki during my stroke recovery. You were the tower of strength she needed while she was pouring so much of herself into me.

To Sue Patience and Norm Jones at the Middlemore Dialysis unit. Sue, thanks for understanding my need to have the freedom to pursue our busy lives and for not demanding that I spend unnecessary hours dialysing or training at the unit. You helped make dialysis easier. And Norm, how many times have you been my on-line "flight instructor" whenever the machine played up, day or night? Thank you for gently guiding me through technical instructions and making repairs quickly and efficiently so that our lives were not too disrupted.

To my parents and siblings for understanding the pressures we feel. To Mum and Dad, your care, love, and support at all times have been invaluable.

To the team in the office, particularly Steve and Leanne Hooper and Joy Sharp. You've had to live with me day in and day out, and cover for me often when events have taken me out of the picture. Thanks for understanding and helping to bear the burden, and for being such loyal, dedicated co-workers.

Thanks to everyone who contributed to making this book come together: Fran and Jonathan Taylor for your excellent proofing, Jenni Smith for your acknowledgments

keen eye for design, Jeff Lord for answering questions and getting us quotes

on printing, and to all the others who encouraged and supported us through

the process.

   And finally, we pay a tribute to our team of faithful personal supporters

who have provided for our family's needs and our ministry, not only

financially but with their encouragement and gift of holidays, etc. What

an incredible blessing you have all been to us. Thank you.

                                                              —Andy Bray

chapter one

one day changes everything

I should have never gone on that ski trip. Little did I know my adventurous life was about to come to a screeching halt.

I was twenty years old, six foot two, youthful, strong, broad-shouldered, virile, and aerobically fit—I had the world at my fingertips. I had a prestigious job as production manager of J. Walter Thompson, a worldwide advertising agency; and I was engaged to Pam—my perfect match—a real adventurous, outdoors, sporty young woman. We were both playing for leading volleyball teams and on the competitive tennis circuit. Nothing could touch me; I loved a challenge. I was an outdoorsman, a Queen Scout, so every weekend it seemed I was either tramping or skiing or canoeing some river. And I lived in the perfect country to do it all, New Zealand. Or as it is sometimes referred to, Godzone.

Maybe it was that sense of invincibility that eventually got me into trouble. I didn't heed my body's warning signals. I was so looking forward to the two-week-long adventure on the slopes of the Southern Alps—some of the best skiing to be found anywhere in the world—with great friends, awesome panoramic views, no crowds, and best of all, great powder. I'd been planning this trip for over a year. So even though I wasn't feeling well, the ski slopes were waiting, and I was determined not to miss out.

Looking back, I guess my doctor should have known better than to release me for the trip; although I have to admit, I did plenty on my part to convince him I would be fine. After all, how bad could a chest cold get? I had strep throat, too, and the doctor wondered if I had pleurisy. But he wasn't sure, and after some persuasion on my part as to how able-bodied I was, he finally told me the words I wanted to hear: "I think you're fine to go."

The rest of the group had gone ahead without me, unsure if I would be able to make it at all. Once "released" by the doctor, I leapt out of my sick bed, got on the next plane, and caught up with them in Christchurch as they were about to maneuver their minivan up the tight-winding roads to the mountains. I wasn't feeling great, but I was determined not to miss out on all the fun.

As I boarded the van, I was greeted with high-fives and shouts of "Hey Andy! Glad you could join us! How are you feeling?"

"I'm fine," I lied, trying to convince myself, too. Little did I know that later in life this was to become my trademark answer to the same never-ending question, *And how are you?* asked of me over and over and over.

"Really? You don't sound too good," they said.

"It's just a little cold. I'm okay. The doctor said I was okay, so here I am." And we left it at that.

Once at the ski lift, our group of eight went up the mountain, two to each chair on the lift. Then, with everybody together at the top, we stood there taking it all in—the warm sun, the crisp, cool mountain air, and the beautiful soft white snow beneath our feet. With shouts of exhilaration and anticipation, the first few in our group began to take off down the hill.

I waited at the back until everyone else had gone on before me; then, with one swift push with my ski poles, I was off. The feeling of freedom was exhilarating. I was gaining speed down the mountain, weaving back and forth, feeling the thrill. What an adrenalin rush! But then halfway down, the rush evaporated away, and I began to feel steadily worse.

My breathing was heavy and strained; my throat was killing me. The whiteness of the slope seemed to spin around me, and my movements felt sluggish and dazed. I felt as though the cold mountain air could blow me over at any moment. Somehow, the strength in my legs had simply vanished—I could hardly hold myself erect.

"Obviously just the aftereffects of a few days in bed," I told myself. "It'll soon wear off." I managed to steer myself off to the side of the slope to keep out of the way of oncoming skiers before I collapsed in the snow, no longer able to support myself. By this point, several people had noticed something was wrong with me; I was lying on the ground, my arms wrapped around my sides, in total exhaustion, and I was unnaturally cold. Involuntary shivers were coursing through my body.

"Hey, you okay mate?" someone shouted.

Nothing like this had ever happened to me before. I was always the one helping others who weren't doing so well. I didn't want to make a scene, so I pretended like it was nothing. "Just catching my breath. Thanks."

The rest of the gang was gone, so after a few moments I summoned what little strength remained, forced myself to my feet, and skied sedately down to our vehicle. Once I finally made it, it took all my strength to pull myself into my sleeping bag and curl up in a ball, feeling sorry for myself and bewildered by this weakness that engulfed me. After a while, the team began to arrive back at the van one by one. I put on a brave face, not wanting to dampen their fun.

"What happened, Andy?" They seemed perplexed at seeing their leader, the one who liked to go down the slopes the fastest, reduced to this shivering wimp, curled up in a sleeping bag while there were ski slopes to conquer. I actually felt quite embarrassed to be caught looking so weak.

"Still getting over this cold, I guess. No worries. I'll come right," I assured them. I put on my best I'm-not-going-to-let-this-sickness-beat-me smile, and we drove off.

Once we were off the mountain, I sought out medical help at a tiny place called Methven, but whatever ailed me was perplexing to the doctor there, too. After listening to my chest and asking some questions, he couldn't really pick up on anything seriously wrong, apart from my strep throat. He, like the doctor back home, didn't caution me against skiing or offer much in the way of advice. So, feeling reassured that I really was okay, I endured the shivering and lack of energy and just pushed myself through the rest of the trip. I knew I wasn't 100 per cent, but as the doctors couldn't diagnose anything, I thought it was just the hangover from my chest cold. "I'll come right," I kept telling myself optimistically.

And I did for awhile. The chest cold improved, my strength returned, and I made the most of our adventure. We went skiing as a group, (a different mountain each day for two weeks), had snow fights, and enjoyed fantastic group time in the evenings—heaps of laughs and great camaraderie. All in all, we considered it a successful, fun trip.

On returning home, I unpacked and settled into my flat. My flatmate was away, so I had the place all to myself for about a week. I crashed on my bed, thankful for the warmth and comfort of a familiar place, and quickly fell asleep.

My dreams were interrupted abruptly when I was awakened in the middle of the night by the most unbelievably excruciating pain. The pain gripped me around the middle of my back so sharply that it made me scream out loud. I couldn't get any relief except by getting a hard object (any hard object), lying down on my back, and pushing myself down on it. The sweat poured off me, and I writhed in agony for two hours. And then... it just subsided. The pain simply vanished as quickly as it had come, and I felt fine again. Weird. I even managed to get back to sleep that night.

Of course, the next morning saw me once again visiting my doctor, who took things more seriously this time and ran some blood tests. My parents and my fiancée, Pam, were starting to feel worried, but none of us knew what to expect. It was then that we found out what had happened: the doctor told me I had chronic renal failure—my kidneys were failing. Apparently the infection from my strep throat had reached my kidneys and attacked them, permanently damaging them—odds of one in ten thousand.

"Basically, here's what happened, Andy," the doctor explained. "You know when you get a cold, you might feel a little bit of pain in your kidneys? Just normal back pain. That's the infection passing through your kidneys. But in your case, as the infection passed through your kidneys in your bloodstream, instead of just passing through, it attacked both kidneys at once."

"And that was the pain I was feeling last night?" I asked.

"Yes. In those two hours, the damage was done. Nothing could have been done to stop it."

I heard what the doctor was saying to me, but it didn't completely register. I certainly didn't understand all the implications it would someday bring. Before I left, the doctor told me I would need to start coming in for regular blood tests so that he could keep an eye on things.

A few weeks later, the doctor called me out of the blue and said, "I'd like to see you. Come into the office and bring your fiancée."

We didn't know why he wanted to see us, but we thought we probably shouldn't skip out on it. We went into his office, took a seat, and hoped he didn't have bad news for us. What if he had found something in my blood tests? He walked in and sat down across from us.

"Hi, Andy. Pam. Thanks for coming today."

We nodded, waiting for him to tell us why we were there.

"Andy." He paused, as if for dramatic effect. "You realise with your blood results, it's likely that you're going to go on dialysis at some point. I just think it would be unwise for the two of you at this point to get married."

I don't know what we expected the doctor to say, but certainly not that. The whole idea seemed completely ridiculous. We were on a roller-coaster ride, and the wedding date had been set. It was the natural course of events to take. Not to mention I felt fine—tired, but fine. Pam and I were still going horseback riding, canoeing, doing all of the things we would normally do, and living a full life. I wasn't really sick.

The doctor must have understood the strain dialysis can have on a marriage. But Pam, who was only nineteen, and I really didn't understand what dialysis meant. I had never even seen a dialysis unit.

The doctor's report had virtually no effect on us. We were more upset by the fact that he charged us for that appointment that *he* invited us to! I wrote him out a cheque, feeling very annoyed with him, and we walked away. Pam and I thought, "This won't happen to us. That doctor doesn't know what he's talking about." So we just pushed everything to the back of our minds and got on with living life. We were engaged to be married, and we had a wedding to organise—not to mention that we needed to focus on making some money fast to pay for it.

We were married a few months later, on the first of June, 1978. After the festivities and plenty of photos, we set off for what ended up being a mildly disastrous honeymoon. As we were driving through mounds of snow on a deserted road around New Zealand's Central Plateau, a helicopter came flying up out of nowhere, and the downrush of air caused a big rock to be thrown right at us, smashing our windscreen. We were miles from anywhere. We had to knock our windscreen out, then unpack and put on all our thermal gear—down jackets, gloves, and hats—and negotiate the white-frosted highway as driving snow came howling at us through the broken windscreen. By the time we pulled into a gas station for repairs about an hour later, we were frozen stiff, and snow had filled the inside of our car, covering our suitcases and belongings.

"It doesn't get much worse than this," I grumbled. Pam was shivering too much to reply.

The owners of the gas station took one look at their bedraggled new arrivals and immediately took pity on us newlyweds. They warmed us up with hot soup and then gave us the bad news.

"It's going to take about five days for a new windscreen to arrive," they said.

We found ourselves stuck in a tiny motel in National Park with our honeymoon itinerary shot to pieces. And to top if off, Pam came down with a terrible cold that drove her to bed for the entire time. I guess I'd looked forward to being in bed with her, but not like this. Some honeymoon. All in all, we were happy to just return home.

Years later, as I look back on the photographs taken during that time, it is evident that I did not look well at all. But at the time, I was totally unaware of how sick I was becoming. And circumstances like the ski trip and the snowy honeymoon were pushing my body further than what it could really handle.

In the weeks after our wedding, I would go on tramping expeditions with the scouts and struggle to keep my normal pace. I had no strength in my legs and no energy, so my response to this was to increase my exercise regime. I didn't understand how I could be so unfit. I was active, so why wasn't my body in good shape? As I increased my work-out time and intensity, I was neglecting to do something the doctor had instructed me to do—take a blood test each month so that he could monitor things. I was very undisciplined about this, and I only got a test done once every three months or so.

I remember going on a canoe adventure over Easter weekend down the Wanganui River with a group of Venturer Scouts. I woke up one morning to discover my eyelids, my nose—my whole face—swollen up like a big balloon. I learnt later that it was caused by fluid retention seeping into my pores because I had slept with my head positioned downhill. Even though we laughed about how ridiculous I looked, the fluid building up in my body was not a good sign.

One day, about six months after the wedding, I was returning to work after visiting a client to get him to approve some artwork. I parked my car in the usual place and stood at the traffic lights, waiting to cross the road. The wind felt so intense on my face I could hardly stand it. Just getting across the road was such an effort. Each step felt as though I was pushing against thousands of pounds of force. I felt impatient and frustrated, but the wind just would not subside. The struggle caused me to breathe so heavily that by the time I made it into the lift, a stranger commented, "You look terrible. Are you alright?" At that point, I really wasn't sure. But I replied, "Oh yeah, I'm just exhausted. Boy, the wind's strong, isn't it?"

"No, it's not too bad, mate."

I arrived in my office, glad to sink down into my office chair to relax, and then the phone rang. It was a renal doctor at the hospital.

"Is this Andy Bray?"

"Yes," I said.

"What are you doing right now?"

"I'm at work."

The doctor paused. "We need to see you right away," he said. "You'd better get in here quick." I left work immediately, fearing the worst but not knowing what the worst might be.

On arriving at the hospital outpatient clinic, the doctor took one look at me and said, "I don't know how you're managing to walk about. These latest blood tests show me that you have no renal function left. You are in serious trouble, young man. We need to prepare you for dialysis."

Immediately I thought, "I can't!" All the things I was organising flashed through my mind. I was the National Rover Advisor, we were getting ready for the National Volleyball Championships, the Tennis Club was building a new clubhouse.

But reality set in—my life was about to change forever. They put me on a bed and wheeled me up to the renal ward to prepare me for an operation to install a fistula into my left arm. I didn't even know what a fistula was. Suddenly I was being bombarded with terminology that was alien to me. Not understanding what was happening to me made it all the more frightening. Unfortunately for me, and because I had missed so many crucial blood tests, my body had rapidly deteriorated without my even knowing about it.

Put simply, a fistula is a graft placed inside the wrist that short-circuits a vein by using an artery to allow greater blood flow to pass through the vessel. In order for me to undergo dialysis, two large needles about the size of a two-inch nail would need to be inserted in the vein each time. A normal vein isn't large enough to handle the needles. The fistula is necessary to make the vein big enough to have sufficient blood flow into a kidney machine. With the fistula installed under local anesthetic (it was an excruciatingly uncomfortable procedure), I was told I would have to wait another six weeks for the fistula to develop before I could begin dialysis.

What a long, dreadful six weeks that was as I waited at home for the fistula to get big enough. I was urinating only a small portion of what I drank. As the fluid built up inside me, the accumulation of toxins began to poison my body. Eventually, I stopped urinating completely. It was impossible to lie down, as the fluid would collect in my lungs and gargle in my throat, making me nauseous. But moving about was out of the question—even the stairway to the lounge was an impossible hurdle for this "invincible man". I found the only way I could sleep was propped up on a bean bag on the floor. Sleep brought intermittent respite, but then only through sheer exhaustion. I could tell my mum and dad were worried about me. And as for me, I was only going through the motions of day-to-day life, just surviving in a haze of illness. I was barely even aware of Pam at this point. I had slipped into survival mode and wasn't conscious of much of anything that was going on around me. But I knew she was worried and probably couldn't help thinking that this was not what she had expected married life to be like.

Finally the day came when I got my first dialysis session. Actually, by then I was so sick that the doctors decided to bring my treatment early, even though my fistula had not grown to the size they would have liked. I was crying out for treatment—the machine was a godsend. Rather than being afraid of it, I just wanted to bring it on. They drained four or five kilos of fluid out of me in a couple of hours, causing severe, painful cramps over my entire body. And the headache afterwards! But it was a relief just to be able to breathe again. The first time Pam came to see me for my dialysis session, she came in, saw me there on the machine, then got a strange look on her face and passed out on the floor. That should have given me a clue that the next couple of years were not going to be easy by any means.

From that point on, I had to go on a kidney machine three times a week for six hours at a time, sometimes even eight hours through the night. Dialysis works like this: You put two needles in your arm. One needle takes blood out and quickly pumps it into a machine where it passes through a man-made kidney thousands of times. Through osmosis, the kidney takes out the toxins and excess fluid in the blood. The clean blood gets pumped back in, along with some extra nutrients, through the second needle. Even so, dialysis only sustains a person at about 40 per cent of the level of a normal kidney. So although I was faithful to my schedule of dialysis, I never felt perfectly well. The dialysis began to take a heavy toll on our marriage.

Just as disheartening as my failing health, the doctor informed me I would never be able to have children. The strain of dialysis, the threat of sterility, and the side effects of these problems, including a loss of libido, became too much for Pam to accept. And to be honest, I was a terrible patient, yelling at the machine or at Pam if something went wrong.

We had been married for about four years when one night we were lying in bed together reading, and Pam said, "I want to tell you something. Put your book down."

So I put my book down and focused my attention on her. She sounded serious. Not angry, but serious.

"I don't want to be married anymore," she said.

Shock was the first emotion I felt. Did she really mean it? It was the last thing I expected her to say after all that we'd been through.

"I can't do this any longer," she continued. "I married an outdoorsman, a sportsman, not a... kidney patient. I love you like a brother, Andy. I don't love you like a husband. And this just isn't what I expected marriage to be like."

My response was one of unbelief. In fact, I smiled at her, saying, "We can sort this out, Pam. We can find some answers. Don't worry."

But she insisted, "No, Andy. I'm serious about this." I could see in her face that she had made up her mind. I was flabbergasted; I didn't know what to say or what to do. I had to clear my head and try to think straight.

I got out of bed, got dressed, and went out to my car. I drove around for hours that night, just crying. I had no idea Pam was so unhappy. We didn't have a great marriage, but we were comfortable with each other. We didn't have major fights or anything, although it's true that we weren't the best at communicating with each other. We'd have lots of silent moments. But I didn't think things were so bad that we needed to get divorced.

Eventually I found myself back home again, begging Pam to reconsider. "Look, I'll do anything. What do I have to do to change?" But it was no use, and I knew it.

"Andy, I promise I'll stay around at least long enough to help you find another way to make dialysis work without me," she said.

Pam knew I relied on her to help me get the machine set up, put the needles in, and assist with all the other little things involved with doing dialysis at home. She kept her promise and stuck around until my parents had learnt enough about dialysis to help me in case of an emergency, but it was not an easy time as it just seemed so strained and false.

During this period, my parents were very supportive, but I was determined to be as independent with the machine as I could to minimise the burden of dialysis on others. And although Mum and Dad were willing to "baby-sit" me, I learnt to dialyse on my own, becoming one of the first in New Zealand to do home dialysis alone.

Needless to say, life wasn't going the way I had planned. I dealt with my discouragement for the next several years by pouring myself into work, sports, and amazing holidays. After a while, I even managed to move past the pain of divorce. Looking back, the years after Pam left me became a selfish time—I was spending a fortune on myself. I kept involved in activities like windsurfing, skiing, and tennis (I was president of the Orakei Tennis Club). I was also a regular attendee at the gym, achieving a level of aerobic fitness despite my dialysis. I entered biathlons and 10km fun runs. I travelled when I had to, plugging into machines at different centres, and I tried my best to live a good life with the kidney machine as my regular companion, keeping me alive.

August 14, 1988 (ten years after my kidneys had failed), started out to be not much different from any other day. My Uncle Wally and Aunt Ruth had stopped by for a visit that evening, and I was sitting at home dialysing and enjoying their company, when the phone rang. It was the hospital, and they said very simply, "Mr Bray, we have a kidney here that's compatible if you're interested. We'll give you two hours to make up your mind."

It might seem that that would be great news and that I would be jubilant. Instead, I was very hesitant, quite unsure how I should respond. You see, five years earlier I had been given a kidney transplant, and it hadn't gone well at all. My body never accepted it, and it just rotted inside me. I became so unwell in a few days that I nearly died as I waited for plasma to be couriered from Australia. Without it the doctors couldn't remove the poisoned graft. When the doctors finally did the surgery to take it out, they said the kidney was like a big, black pudding that had grown inside me. It had been a scary time, a major setback, and my recovery after that pointless episode took months. So needless to say, I had some reservations about trying again. But at the same time,

I realised it was my only hope, my only opportunity for living a normal, healthy life.

My Uncle Wally agreed that I couldn't pass up the opportunity. "It's a no-brainer. You have to do it. Go for it!" he said.

So after some careful thought, I called back and said, "Okay. I'll do it."

It seems any time I go to the hospital, there's some kind of complication. After racing to get there in time, I found the operation had to be delayed twenty-four hours because a badly mangled water-skier had been admitted after a speedboat ran over him and the motor had literally ripped his guts out. They had to do a six-hour operation to patch him up. Meanwhile, my new kidney sat in the ice, so it wasn't fresh anymore by the time they got around to putting it in. I'm sure that added to the complications that were to follow.

Quite often during a kidney transplant, the surgeons can visibly see blood flowing into the new graft and urine almost immediately beginning to be made. This didn't happen in my case. In fact, I had to wait three weeks before my body accepted the kidney. In that time, I had to continue with dialysis, and I became very discouraged with every passing day of no function.

For six nights I also had to endure a nightmarish treatment of an anti-rejection drug apparently made from rat serum called OKT3. Each night they would give me this drug and I would dread having to shut my eyes. Now I know where directors get their ideas for horror movies. The bed seemed to hover off the ground, white surgeon gloves floated towards me, and the room turned strange flashing colours and moved around me in a whirl. I hated every moment of it.

Then finally one night I felt some excruciating pain in my belly, and one of the night registrars came to check on me.

"It really hurts," I groaned. "I don't know what's wrong."

"Hmm," he said. "Let's try putting this catheter in and see what happens." He hooked it up, and *whoosh*! The bag attached to the catheter immediately filled up with urine, and I felt amazing. The kidney was working! From that day on, as each family member paid a visit we celebrated together as we watched the golden flow of urine down the tube. Never had there been so much excitement over the ability of one man to pee!

Despite early complications, receiving that transplant was incredible—like being reborn. When the transplant began functioning, all of my senses were sharpened. I felt alive and vibrant. I could feel my fingerprints—the sensitivity of my touch was electric. I could see and hear with clarity. I felt like Superman, ready to take on the world. Energy was vibrating through me. From being sick for so long, it was a dramatic change. I hadn't even realised how much my body had deteriorated until I felt like a normal person again.

And the real truth of it all dawned on me: while we were celebrating this new life, elsewhere another family was in mourning over the death of their loved one. Someone I didn't know had died in a car accident, but that person's death meant that I would receive this kidney. Little did I know this concept of someone else's death for my life would become an analogy for something even greater that would happen to me very soon.

chapter two

a second chance

As the kidney began to work, I needed to have a few minor operations to sort things out inside. I hadn't been able to urinate for ten years, so a few things had stopped working down below. Although urine was now flowing, it was excruciatingly painful, but things slowly began to sort themselves out. Funny thing though: I needed to go every couple of hours, so whenever I travelled anywhere with my family or friends, I was always checking out the toilet facilities (or at least ensuring a tree was handy).

The medical care was quite intensive following the transplant. I paid visits to the hospital every day for about three months and had regular blood tests to ensure that all rejection phases were nipped in the bud. "We don't count the transplant a success until you've reached the one-year mark," one doctor explained to me. "So these monthly tests are vital."

I learnt that even after the one-year mark, the monthly tests would still be important. A transplant recipient can never really be confident that the graft will keep going—the body can reject it at any time. It's an emotional roller-coaster ride as you hope your blood tests and creatinine levels stay normal.

"Because of this high chance of rejection, you'll need to take some doses of steroids and some anti-rejection drugs in the first six months or so until we're confident enough to wean you off them," the doctor said. So now that I had the chance to finally feel well, I had no choice but to take handfuls of highly toxic drugs that made me feel lousy all over again. The "getting better" process seemed to take forever.

After some time, things did improve and I began to feel incredible. I noticed how clean I was inside without any toxins present, and I suddenly felt as though I could do anything.

A sense of thankfulness engulfed me. And then, being reminded I didn't know how long this kidney would work, I began to reflect on my options. I realised I had a chance for a new life. I wanted to make the most of every moment.

I threw myself into my life with a new gusto. I had a confidence about me that grew into arrogance as I enjoyed my new "superhuman" strength. I must have been a right pain to be around. I even remember my sister slipping me a friendly note subtly telling me that I was too cocky. But I was bouncing off walls, unable to contain all this new energy. I said to myself, "Doesn't everyone else feel this way?"

I went back to work at my job as a director at Insight Communications, a leading design business started by my brother-in-law, Mike Tisdall. I enjoyed working with Mike, a talented individual with a gift for design. He was quick at grasping complex business issues and helping clients communicate their own business to the public. Despite the huge pressure of the job, it was a thrill to be involved in a thriving, successful business with a very formidable blue-chip client base that included the likes of Air New Zealand and Lion Nathan.

All in all, life was once again going pretty well. And although I was very cocky and proud on the outside, the transplant had another effect on me: having been given a second chance at life somehow made me more introspective. Was I happy with my life? Was there perhaps more to life than I was experiencing? I wasn't sure, but I wanted to find out.

It was soon after this point, when I was feeling like a new person on top of the world, that I began to find the answers to some of my questions. It all started when I met a fun-loving, attractive woman from England named Nikki.

There I was one morning at work with a million things to do, as usual, when this pretty young representative from Spicer Cowan Papers came to see me.

"Hello, I'm Nikki," she introduced herself. Her accent clearly identified her as British.

"Hi," I said, shaking her hand. "So, you work for Spicer Cowan?"

"Yes," she said. "It's my first week with the company." She held up the company's credit card and continued, "We have a box at the Benson and Hedges Tennis Open and I've been instructed to invite our top clients to join me there. Would you be interested in coming?"

Well, it's a tough job, but I guess someone has to do it. The offer was too fantastic for me to pass up. I took the day off work and was ushered into a private box at courtside where Nikki was ready to play hospitality, prepared to order me anything I wanted for the day.

"Champagne? Strawberries and cream?" she asked.

"Sure!" I said. Even with great service and world-class tennis action, I admit I was much more intrigued by Nikki than the game. Nikki's physical attractiveness did not slip past me. She was a pretty English girl with blonde hair, bright eyes, a big accent, and a big smile, but something that captivated me even more were the things she told me about herself.

"What do you like to do in your spare time?" I asked her, trying to generate a conversation.

"I like to work with youth," she replied.

"Youth? What youth?"

"The youth group at my church."

"Oh, so you go to church, do you?" I said, a bit cynically. I'd never met anyone who went to church because they wanted to. My parents dragged me to church when I was a kid, and I hated it. As soon as they said I didn't have to go anymore, I stopped going completely.

"Sure, it's a great church. I love church," she said. She could see my surprise. "I'm a Christian," she explained boldly.

I was intrigued. I peppered her with questions all day long. I truly wanted to understand what she believed and why. She was so sure about her life and where she was going. I found that aspect of her personality irresistible. Because I had received my transplant six months earlier, I was feeling awesome about life, but I was also searching for, well, something more—a whole lot more.

She had gotten my attention, that's for sure, but romance was out of the question. For one thing, she was way too young for me—twenty-one—which made her ten years younger. And with the breakup of my previous marriage, there was no way I was going down that path again! But there was something about Nikki that made me want to spend more time with her.

After the match, I invited Nikki to play tennis with me at the tennis club. She accepted, and we had a great time hanging out in a non-romantic context, just enjoying each other's company. Because we shared an interest in tennis, horseback riding, and the outdoors, we began spending time together and became friends quickly. I found I wanted to learn as much as I could about her faith—something about it gripped me.

I even started going to church with Nikki regularly (which wasn't at all like the churches I remembered growing up). Nikki took her faith seriously and she had made it very clear to me up front that as she was a Christian and I wasn't, she had absolutely no interest in being anything more than good friends. That was fine with me; I had made up my mind that I wouldn't marry again anyway.

In getting to know her and learning about her faith, then reading about Christ in the Bible, it wasn't long until I began to reflect on my own life. I realised just how selfish and sinful I had become: totally self-absorbed, doing whatever I wanted to do, whenever I wanted to do it. My life was all about me. My sister was right: I had become cocky. I began to understand I needed Christ in my life.

The overwhelming sense of my need began to grow. Finally, one Sunday night when I was at an evening church service with Nikki, I just felt a strong urge to get my life right before God. I would have been too intimidated to go to the front for one of those "altar calls", but luckily the pastor had something else in mind.

At the end of his sermon, he announced, "If this service has touched your heart and raised some questions and you'd like someone to pray with you, come and meet me out back." That appealed to me. I could go out the back. That wasn't too hard.

I spoke with the pastor after the service and explained what was going on in my heart.

"I feel like there's something more to life," I said. "I want what Nikki's got. I think I need Christ in my life."

"Would you like me to pray with you?" the pastor asked.

So that night I prayed and told Jesus that I needed Him in my life. It wasn't a radically emotional experience, but once I finished praying, I felt fantastic. I knew there was something different about me. I didn't know it then, but that moment was to be the catalyst to a radically changed life.

I came back to Nikki with a huge grin on my face. "I'm a Christian!" I told her.

It's a moment that is etched vividly in my mind, more vividly in fact than receiving my transplant. And it was at that moment that I realised two profound things about my new-found faith that my transplant mirrored: The first was that someone had to die for me so that I could have renewed life. The second was that it wasn't until I became well that I realised just how sick I had really become.

My new faith was to become a springboard into a life that was more meaningful than I could ever imagine. Radical changes began to take place in my life almost immediately. My outlook was different; my reason for being was different. I wanted God to use my life, no matter how long or short it was, to make an impact.

Having a personal relationship with Christ made all the difference. When I was young, I hated church because it was all about reading and memorising boring rites and liturgies, mumbling through old-fashioned hymns, and listening to the monotone drone from the pulpit. It had seemed like a boring waste of time. But once I learnt that Christianity was about a person who had a direct impact and interest in my life, my new church experience was completely different. The people were passionate and excited; the preaching was meaningful and topical; the worship was an uplifting celebration. The Bible no longer seemed like something dark and dour, full of rules. It was a bright and exciting manual that made one free to live a brilliant plan—a guide to living life to the full!

My perspective on church wasn't the only thing that changed. Once I took that step and accepted Jesus into my heart, Nikki and I began to see each other in new and fresh ways. I began to truly look forward to meeting her for Bible studies and devotions together, as I longed to know more about God and grow with her. I became enamored with this wonderful woman who had a profound sense of purpose. In the midst of this, despite the caution we each felt about a relationship, romance blossomed naturally. It quickly became evident to both of us that God had a plan for us to be together.

Several months later, on July 10, I took Nikki on a ski trip for her birthday. Over breakfast that morning, I handed her an old photographic box.

"What's this?" she asked.

"Just open it," I replied.

She opened the box and could see a pile of jigsaw pieces. She didn't have to look very hard to realise the jigsaw had been created from a picture of us. "Oh, it's a jigsaw of us that you've had made. How nice." She closed the box and smiled. "Are you ready to go skiing?"

Actually, I wanted her to put the puzzle together right away, but the snow was beckoning louder than my silly jigsaw, so we left it sitting on the table while we went skiing for the day.

When we returned several hours later, I begged her to do the puzzle with me. Nikki must have wondered about my impatience to put the jigsaw together, but there really was a method to my madness. "Oh, alright," she said, resigning herself that she wouldn't hear the end of it until she had completed the puzzle.

We sat down together and worked away on it until it was finally finished, revealing a handsome photo of the two of us.

"Now turn the puzzle over," I instructed.

"What? I don't understand."

"Just turn it over. Here, let me help."

I put the lid on top and gently lifted the puzzle. Very carefully, we turned it over upside down and removed the lid. Imprinted on the back of the jigsaw puzzle were the words, "Nikki, I love you. Please marry me!"

She looked up at me, surprised but clearly happy, and said, "Yes!"

Before going off to celebrate, I said, "And if our marriage is ever in pieces, we can sit down and put it back together again." I didn't know then how many times we would actually have to do that in the early years of our marriage.

In fact, we even experienced some ups and downs during our engagement. One of those times that I remember vividly occurred when we became heavily occupied in something that was a bit of a blessing and a curse at the same time—we organised the very first New Zealand team to compete in the World Transplant Olympics.

One of the many things I had read in my hospital bed while I waited for my new kidney was a brochure by the International Kidney Society on the World Transplant Games, an event designed to showcase the success of transplantation to the world.

It was an international sporting event for transplant recipients, proving that a transplant provides such amazing health improvements that transplant patients can compete athletically on a worldwide level.

The next World Transplant Games were to take place in Singapore in late 1989, less than one year away.

I had to go. I was determined to go. Years ago, before my kidneys had failed, I felt I'd had a good chance of someday representing my country at the Olympics in volleyball. In fact, Pam got even closer, actually getting selected for the top New Zealand squad. Although that dream had been destroyed when my kidneys failed, it was alive once more. Unfortunately, as I made enquiries, I discovered that a New Zealand team had never competed at the games, and there was no organisation that was interested or that had the manpower or funding to make it happen. If I were to compete in the games, I'd have to make it happen myself. So I did. In one sense, it was an amazing experience. Nikki and I, along with my parents and my sister Rosemary, raised all of the money and invited other Kiwis with transplants to come with us. We had a team of twelve that represented New Zealand for the first time ever at the Transplant Games in Singapore. The team nominated me to carry the New Zealand flag into the stadium, and it was quite an emotional and powerful time.

We were a diverse group of athletes: some were good enough to represent their country at the Commonwealth Games—they could run the 100-meter sprint in ten seconds; other athletes were in wheelchairs. We witnessed incredible feats of athleticism. There were at least 1,500 athletes there, and we would see groups of them sitting around the swimming pool in the evenings comparing their scars and stories. One man we talked to had problems with his lungs, so he'd had a heart-lung transplant. But his heart was just fine, so they gave it to someone else. He sat in the stadium with his new lungs and watched the guy who had been given his heart run around the track.

So I was having a great time, and our team did really well—we ended up coming in sixteenth in the world overall, which was an amazing first effort for a very small team. But for some reason, I kept feeling very irritated with Nikki. She would cling to me when I was trying to attend meetings and hanging out with other athletes. She suddenly seemed very young to me—too young. But I didn't understand what was really going on, although she tried to explain it to me.

"People with transplants have a kind of cliquish thing about them," she told me. "You all have this common experience; you have a bond because of what you've been through, and I just feel really out of place."

I wasn't too concerned that she was feeling ostracised. It was true that Nikki was suddenly on her own a lot. We had gone from having a great courtship back home, where we were always doing things together, to the Transplant Games, where I was often with the other athletes and Nikki was left with the other spectators in the stadium. A heavy tension developed between us for the entire trip.

By the time we reached Auckland, we were both thinking the same thing in the back of our minds: "Have we made the right decision? Should we really get married?"

At the airport, she left with her mum and I left with my parents, but I had a horrible, heavy feeling in my heart. I missed Nikki. And I knew deep down that we were right for each other and that we could work out our differences. It was the first of many times that we would let each other down; but each time we worked out our problems, it brought us closer together in a "oneness" relationship.

One of the reasons Nikki had promised herself that she would never marry a non-Christian was that she desired this kind of "oneness" relationship, where we would each strive for similar goals and look to God for wisdom and guidance in our relationship. She knew she would miss out on that if she married a non-Christian, so she made a commitment that she would wait for God's best plan for her life.

Nikki described it to me later. "I didn't just want to marry a Christian," she said. "I wanted to marry someone who was passionate about his relationship with God. I saw myself running towards the finish line—that was me running my Christian faith. And I wanted someone who could keep up. I didn't want someone dragging behind that I had to go back and carry all the time." So I had a lot of running to do to catch up. But God gave me that kind of passion for Him, so it wasn't long before Nikki and I were on a level playing field.

Six months after the Transplant Games, we were married. A song we played at our wedding was called "You, Me and Jesus" by Cliff Richard (1980). Part of the chorus goes like this:

You, me, and Jesus

Jesus, me and you;

On our own we'd break,

With Him we'll make it through.

This whole idea of oneness together and with God was a new concept for me. One plus one plus one equals one. But it made sense—God was the one who designed marriage to work that way, so He could provide the tools to make it possible.

One way I've seen this work in our marriage is that having a spiritual connection has allowed us to be able to truly receive each other as God's gift and provision. I can illustrate this point with one of our favourite memories together—our honeymoon.

Nikki and I originally planned a three-week holiday for our honeymoon. Then during one of our Bible studies together, I read in Deuteronomy that when a man got married, he was to take a year off, not go to work, and delight his wife. I took that literally; and although we couldn't afford an entire year, I changed our honeymoon from three weeks to three months, then to six months. A six-month-long trip was a great way to get to know each other better as we traveled around the world, living in a little tent most of the time.

We traveled from Hawaii and sunshine to Austria for skiing, then to the United Kingdom to tour Nikki's hometown. From there, we hopped on a boat to France, saw Paris at night, and enjoyed cycling and wine tasting (not a wise idea in combination). We went on to Switzerland, then Austria again, and then Italy. We caught a boat to Greece and stayed with friends in Athens. Then our honeymoon got a little bit frightening.

When we told our friends that we had made plans to go to Yugoslavia, they warned us about the dangerous drive ahead.

"There's a civil war going on in Albania," our friends explained. "So whatever you do, be very careful. There are tanks everywhere; the whole army is out and about. You'll need to go across the border, and then it's about an eight-hour drive through the mountains to the coast. And most importantly, do not stop. Drive the whole way, and don't stop or get out of your car at all. It's not safe."

They made us nervous enough that we assured them we would heed their advice.

"One more thing," they said to us just before we left. "Be careful of little kids selling fruit on the side of the road. They're not innocent. If you pull over to buy something from them, hundreds of kids will come out of the trees and swarm you. They'll surround you and take everything."

It was difficult to say what we were more afraid of—military tanks and men with loaded guns or the children. We were hopeful that we wouldn't have a close encounter with either. We drove all day and into the night (thirteen hours total) surrounded by pick-pocket scavengers outside along the way. When we finally arrived in Yugoslavia, it was late at night, but we were thankful we'd made it through okay.

"I'm so tired," Nikki said. "Let's just stop at the next camping ground we come to." So we did. There was no one at the campground office, just a drop box where we could leave our money. We found a camping spot, pitched our tent in the dark, and went to sleep.

In the morning, we decided to go out and explore our surroundings because we had been able to see very little of it the night before. The beach was stunning. We went and had a look at the changing rooms next, and we were surprised to see that there were no doors. The showers were open and so were the toilets—no doors at all.

We walked over to the office, and there was still no one there. However, we saw a framed photograph of the previous year's swimming competition, and all of the competitors in the photo were completely naked!

"That's a bit weird," I said to Nikki. We shrugged and began wandering back to our tent.

By then, a few campers started to come out of their tents, and none of them were wearing clothes!

"Honey, they haven't got any clothes on," I said, trying to avert my eyes.

"Yes, I kind of noticed that," said Nikki.

"I think we're at a nudist camp," I said in amusement. I looked around and noticed the volleyball courts and trampolines, and I couldn't help thinking, "There's no way I would use that stuff in the nude. A trampoline—*imagine...* "

It was really a beautiful, warm day, and because we were the only ones wearing clothes, I actually began to feel a bit conspicuous.

"I think I'll take my clothes off, too," I said to Nikki.

She raised an eyebrow at me. "Well, I'm not," she said, very determined.

"Come on," I said, beginning to strip off. "When in Rome, do as the Romans do." But Nikki refused to take her clothes off, being the nice Christian girl she was and a proper English girl on top of that. So I took off my clothes and sat down outside our tent to read. Fine with me if Nikki wanted to be the only one in the whole place with clothes on.

Before long, some German tourists drove up. They had three kids with them and parked their car directly across from us. In addition, they were all wearing clothes. Suddenly the situation went from Nikki being the only one with clothes to me being the only one without clothes.

I looked around frantically, thinking, "Where are my clothes? Oh no, I left them in the tent!" I used my book to try to cover myself.

The Germans finally addressed us. "This is our campsite. We camp here every year."

"Oh, yeah?" I said, squirming. "You want this campsite?"

"Oh, would you mind?" they said. "We'd really like to stay at this campsite. This is our favourite campsite."

"So you'd like us to move?" I asked. "Now?" Yep, that was what they wanted. But I wasn't moving my book for anybody. Somehow I maneuvered my way back to the tent, so embarrassed that I was hoping I could take it down from the inside. It didn't help that Nikki thought the whole situation was marvelously hilarious. I think she felt that I kind of deserved what I got.

All in all, our honeymoon was a bit wilder than we had anticipated. Nikki could have decided then and there that she'd had enough of this fruitcake who was dragging her all over Europe through dangerous mountains and nudist camps, but she chose to receive me completely—oddities and imperfections included. Nikki didn't know before we got married what I might get her into—on the honeymoon or for the rest of our lives together. Still, she has faithfully chosen love and acceptance throughout the years, and this is not always an easy task! Believe me, I've done worse than leading her into a nudist camp. Lucky for me, Nikki has always been naturally accepting and forgiving.

Although we were slowly learning what it would take to make our marriage last, as newlyweds we still had a long way to go, and we were going to need our marriage to be strong if we were going to make it through the coming years.

chapter three

a calling

Nikki and I were conscious that, considering our backgrounds, our marriage was a recipe for disaster. I had already been divorced from Pam; and although Nikki had never been married, she had a "colourful" background.

Nikki's mother, Deana, came from a dysfunctional Irish family living in England where she was one of sixteen children. She ran away from home at age sixteen to join the Royal Air Force, where she married Nikki's father. The relationship was tumultuous, and Nikki was only four when her parents divorced. Deana needed to take some time to sort herself out, so she placed Nikki and her older brother in an Air Force children's home for awhile. When Deana returned for them, she brought with her a man whom she eventually married.

Nikki loved her stepfather, but that marriage also ended after a few years when he had an affair. A year later, when Nikki was fourteen, Deana met a New Zealand man and later moved out to New Zealand to live with him. Nikki was doing well in school and didn't want to leave her hometown, so she boarded with guardians. The guardians weren't relatives, but they were a lovely, wealthy family with two other children. However, they also divorced three years after Nikki moved in with them. Nikki began to think she must be contributing some sort of bad luck to the failing marriages around her.

The British government labelled Nikki an "abandoned child" because her mother was now living in New Zealand and her father was somewhere in the United Kingdom. As such, she was given a grant to attend York University. While at University, a group of young Christians befriended her, taking a genuine interest in her unique circumstances. She was taken by their passion, purpose, and self-confidence—everything she lacked in her own life. Their love for life and for others made Christianity an attractive proposition to Nikki. One day she prayed, "God, if you're real, I need you to come and make a difference in my life, too." Nikki's life had been tough, and her relationship with Jesus finally provided some stability. It was trustworthy and authentic.

Still, because of her background, Nikki did not have a lot of plans for falling in love and getting married someday. She'd seen too many marriages fall apart and the devastation it caused—particularly to the children. God did a work in both of our hearts to bring us together, but once we were together we had an even more challenging task ahead of us: staying together.

It seems that when couples choose to marry, they automatically assume their marriage will soar and they won't have any problems. I think that newlyweds are a lot like the airplane we bought in a Los Angeles mall on the last leg of our honeymoon. The shopping center we visited was absolutely huge—probably the biggest one I've ever been in. At the bottom floor in the atrium area was a guy who had a polystyrene aircraft with a three-foot-long fuselage, and a big crowd of people had gathered around to watch him do stunts with it.

Nikki and I stopped to watch, too, and we were amazed. This guy could throw the airplane and make it come back to him, then catch it. He would make it loop-the-loop and fly way up high. It blew me away, all the tricks he could do.

"I have to get one of those!" I told Nikki.

"It is amazing, isn't it?" she replied.

So, like scores of others, I paid my money and walked out of the shopping center, the proud owner of the coolest toy ever. The airplane came in a long plastic bag. "I guess there's some assembly required," I said. But I couldn't wait to get home, put it together, and try it out. I had some trouble fitting it into the overhead lockers on our plane, but in the end I managed to squeeze it in.

We got home from our trip, and I was so excited to finally get this thing in the air. I attached the wings and the tail and all the other little parts, being very careful to do it just right. Finally, the moment had come: I picked up the airplane, pulled my arm back, and propelled it forward with a good, solid push. The airplane immediately did a nose dive and crumpled on the ground. The wings popped off during the crash.

Nikki and I picked up the pieces. "Hmmm, that didn't go so well," she said.

"We'll make it work this time," I said confidently.

We put it back together and tried again. And this time... it crashed again. After a bit of trial and error, we finally got it to where we could make it fly back and forth between us. But as for making it loop-the-loop or do other fancy tricks—no way, not like the guy in the mall. Tired of making all the adjustments each time, we put the plane back in its plastic bag and put it away in the garage. As far as I know, it's still there to this day.

I say that this airplane is much like newlyweds because we all start out with such high hopes for marriage. We assume that marriage will be wonderful and that ultimately we'll soar. But when two people come together, it's necessary that they make a number of adjustments, which they're willing to do... for awhile. The marriage might fly okay at first, but if you want it to loop-the-loop and dance and do amazing things, you've got to hang in there, work hard, and keep putting it back together when it gets a little broken. That's when a lot of people give up. They don't have the tools they need, or decide it's just too much work. So they settle for what's easiest or most comfortable, just getting by with flying from one place to the other when the marriage could do so much more.

By the time we got engaged, we both had a strong desire to make our marriage "soar", but we knew the odds were against us. We knew we needed to do everything we could to ensure that our marriage would make it. We made a commitment to each other that every year we would go to some kind of marriage course. Having been through one divorce, there was no way I could bear another.

Just after we hit our two-year milestone, I came home from work and Nikki told me she wanted to show me something.

"What is it?" I asked.

She pulled out an pink piece of photocopy paper that was advertising an upcoming FamilyLife Marriage Conference in Auckland. The "brochure" was type-written with no pictures. Considering I was in the marketing and advertising business doing top ads for top clients and magazines, I was not impressed.

"I don't think so," I told her. "I can't imagine that's any good. I mean, look at it; we'll probably be sleeping in bunks in a church camp." I had in my mind a low-budget, disorganised operation run by a couple of geriatrics—not my idea of an enjoyable way to spend my time.

"I think it would be good for us to go to it," Nikki persisted. "We did make a decision to do things like this. Just give it a try; it won't be so bad. It does say it's at the Waipuna Hotel."

Inwardly groaning, I finally agreed to go because I'd made a commitment to her, but I was not looking forward to it. Nikki called and registered us for the conference, and I made up my mind to just make the best of it. It was only one weekend.

On arrival we discovered the conference was actually held in the hotel's four-star theatre. I walked in and began to relax—this didn't look so bad after all. We arrived early to sign in, then sat down in the auditorium near the very front. There were about forty other couples there. A large screen was set up at the front so that we could watch the conference; it was all on video.

One of the speaker couples on the video was Dennis and Barbara Rainey, co-founders of FamilyLife in the United States. Dennis was clearly a man of conviction and he was humble enough to share his mistakes. As I watched them on the video, I found out that they were a young couple with six kids who were struggling with the pressures of marriage and family just like all of us. Dennis was extremely humorous. Some of the situations and stories he shared were so funny because they were so true to our lives, too.

After only one session, I was hooked. I kept thinking, "This is something *everyone* needs to hear!" The speakers were talking about issues I could really relate to, sharing their experiences with an obvious passion for marriages, and including humour in a professional environment. We were learning new things every lesson. We thought we had a good marriage, but Nikki and I acknowledged that day that we were living well short of what was possible. We had been sucked in by our culture's lifestyle without realising it, trapped in the world's mindset of materialism, selfishness, and independence, not knowing we had been setting ourselves up for failure. Now we had a refreshed marriage, a bigger vision, and a plan we could use that would work. I wanted to fly to Little Rock and join Dennis Rainey and FamilyLife right then.

Although flying to Little Rock right away was probably out of the question, we knew that I could at least help the FamilyLife team in New Zealand produce a better brochure. I couldn't let this awesome conference get by with such pathetic marketing. My office was equipped with the latest gear and best designers, so I knew it would be easy to add value.

I invited the FamilyLife staff to our board room and threw around some ideas involving money. I had plans to produce a brochure that would be multi-colored, glossy, and folded in twenty-five places. I admit I was even a bit arrogant, basically telling them how they should run their ministry.

"Look, you have a fantastic conference, but lousy marketing. You need to add a lot more sizzle to the sausage," I said frankly.

Bob Helvey, the FamilyLife director in New Zealand, was humble and glad to accept my services. "But we don't have much money," he cautioned. I had to settle for designing a one-color brochure, but I was excited to be involved even in this small way in what they were doing.

It wasn't long before Nikki and I became involved with organising and helping promote the conferences. The cream on the cake was being asked to go to the conferences to help throughout the weekend. It was an awesome time for us. We were active and busy, and we were seeing how God was using these events to change lives and marriages, including our own.

The first conference we attended inspired us by presenting us with a goal and a standard. But it was from hearing the message over and over that it really started to sink in.

Resolving conflict, for example, was a big issue for us. Because of Nikki's background, she had always seen conflict as a sign that things weren't going right. And when things weren't going right, people got divorced—that had been her observation. So she tended to run away from conflict, whereas I liked to charge in and fight it out. Besides, I could be a great prosecuting attorney when I wanted to, and I could twist her words to confuse her and win points. We learnt that instead of trying to win an argument, we needed to approach confrontation lovingly and be quick to grant forgiveness. We even came to enjoy our disagreements in a way by trying to see our views from each other's perspective, and Nikki learnt that because I often affirmed my lifetime commitment to her, she never had to fear that I might leave her when conflicts arose. Many other essentials to a good marriage were ingrained in our minds as we heard the message presented dozens of times.

I distinctly remember sitting in the conference and hearing the principle about "receiving your partner as a gift from God Himself". It quickly dawned on me how I hadn't really done this. I saw that I was dominating Nikki in so many subtle ways. I was using my age (ten years older) and maturity to influence her; I was using my size (twelve inches taller) in a subtle way to get what I wanted; and I was maximising my role as the head of the home.

Right away I understood what I had been doing without really realising it. I instantly decided to change and be more proactive at making sure Nikki felt heard, and to ensure that we were operating in an equal partnership. It proved to be a key to turning our marriage around and it helped us fly higher off the ground. What amazed me most was how Nikki began to grow so much in confidence and as a woman that I found myself becoming more and more proud of her every day.

We were seeing other lives and marriages change, too. I once spoke with a marriage therapist who told me that one of the first things he tried to do when couples came to him for counselling was to get them to attend a FamilyLife Weekend to Remember marriage conference.

"If I can do that," he said, "I can cut six months off of their counselling experience with just this one weekend. It's the best jumpstart we can do."

We heard stories of couples on the brink of divorce whose lives were turned around. One couple's marriage had been destroyed by drugs and affairs. They attended the conference, and God turned their marriage around so that you wouldn't even recognise them as the same couple today. They are now so in love and thrilled that their family is still intact, yet very aware at just how broken their lives could have been. They began helping others to build their marriages by getting involved with promoting and organising conferences along with us.

At this point in our lives, another exciting development was taking place that gave us a new incentive to keep our marriage strong. Remember when the doctor told me I would be unable to have children? Turns out he was wrong! It seemed that we just had to *think* about children and it happened. We had three children in five years: Natasha, Olivia, and Ben. It's hard to describe the feeling, after having been told that I couldn't have children, of coming home from work and seeing a toddler come running toward me with arms open wide, yelling "Daddy!

Daddy!" Wow. People take certain expectations for granted because it's easy to get married, and it's usually easy to have kids. But it seemed to me almost like a reward. It was an amazing blessing for me and Nikki. I'm reminded every time I see them that with God all things are possible.

On more than one occasion, I got down on my knees before each of my children and said, "I'm so thankful that God chose me to be your dad! What a lucky man I am!"

Before long, we were faced with a decision of whether or not to continue trusting God to make possible what seemed to us impossible. I had a stable, high-paying job, but I was beginning to feel the disillusionment of working in the corporate world. I felt there were no ways for me to really serve God there. The things I could see happening through FamilyLife were so much more life-changing and exciting than handing a project to a client who's worried about a spelling mistake on page three.

Casually, I said things to Nikki from time to time like, "What do you think about doing this FamilyLife thing full-time?"

Her answer was always, "We can't. We need to make a living."

I couldn't argue. How would I possibly be able to support us if I quit my job? And although I loved FamilyLife, would I really be willing to give up a lucrative salary, a company car, and all the trimmings for a life in ministry? I felt like I was being pulled in two different directions.

Finally, one day Nikki felt that the Lord was saying to her, "Stop holding back." She came to me and said, "If this is something you really want to do, I'll trust that God will provide for the family. I'm right behind you."

That was all I needed. With the support of my wife behind me and God on our side, I handed in my notice at work the very next day. Nikki was a little surprised by the suddenness.

"You could give me a little time to get used to the idea!" she said.

As full-time ministry staff, we were required to raise all of our salary. This process was a bit intimidating at first—calling people, setting up appointments to share our vision for strengthening marriages and families throughout New Zealand and ask for money. It wasn't easy, especially as we didn't have too many contacts. Nikki was new to the country and I'd been a Christian for only one year. We trusted by faith that if God was calling us to FamilyLife, He would provide the funds we needed to make it possible. In fact, it gave us a chance to see God work as we witnessed His faithfulness and provision through generous friends.

We had one appointment with a successful, dynamic businessman who was a very bottom-line kind of guy. Fortunately, we'd invited him and his wife to our conference, and they'd come and had a very positive experience. I'm sure that helped, but we were not prepared for what was about to happen. We came into his office and he said in a friendly but direct way, "You've got five minutes. Tell me what the story is."

With our design and marketing backgrounds, we had developed a slick, professional presentation, but we couldn't do it in five minutes. So we had to throw the presentation out the window.

"Well, here's what we need," I began, pulling out a financial summary.

"I don't want to hear what you need," he interrupted me. "Tell me what you want."

"Oh, okay," I said, a bit unsure of myself now, and feeling quite intimidated. "Well, we need $360 a month... "

"No, no. I know what your needs are. Tell me what you *want*. I'll tell you what: I'm going to leave the room for five minutes so you can talk about it. When I come back, I want you to tell me what you want. What do you want to leave here with?" And he got up and left the room.

A few minutes later, he came back. "Alright. What is it?"

"Well, we need... "

"Don't tell me what you need. Tell me what you want."

"Okay. We'd like $1,000 a month towards our salary and $4,000 for a new computer and printer for the office."

Without hesitation, he got out his cheque book and wrote out $5,000 on the spot and handed me the cheque. "There's your computer, and your first $1,000 installment. And I can't see any reason why that should ever have to stop."

We were speechless. I showed the cheque to Bob Helvey later that week. "We can buy a new computer—look!" And to this day, that man has kept his word and never missed one monthly installment.

Although initially we had to make some drastic adjustments to a much smaller family budget, and raising support to join FamilyLife was a bit intimidating and required tenacity and perseverance, it was amazing to see God answer our prayers as He provided us with financial and prayer partners who believed in what we were doing and who combined to provide us with a salary equal to that of a secondary school teacher. Instances such as our meeting with the businessman were confirmation to us that we were where God wanted us to be.

We had only been on staff for eight or nine months when we received some news we weren't prepared for. Bob and Kathy Helvey invited us on a picnic one afternoon and said they had something to tell us.

"We're so glad you and Nikki are here. While we would love to stay here in New Zealand with you, we need to go back to FamilyLife in the States. We've been waiting for God to raise up a Kiwi couple to be in charge."

Nikki and I were devastated. We were new on staff, and I was still growing as a Christian. We were not equipped to take over the ministry. We were also disappointed because one of the reasons we joined the ministry was to work alongside Bob and Kathy. Apart from being highly organised and wonderful spiritual mentors, they had become our best friends, and we would miss them terribly. Bob often gave me good advice and was helping me develop better disciplines and habits in my life as a man, husband, and father. And we just didn't feel ready for the responsibility of directing the ministry. Again, we had to trust God that if this was what He wanted us to do, He would give us the ability to do it. We accepted the role, as there was no one else to do it.

We felt strongly about building strong marriages and families because the world, and more specifically, our country, was (and still is) a mess— youth suicides, broken marriages, child abuse. We needed God. Nikki and I felt that FamilyLife was the best way to spread the message of hope, but we began to find there were other benefits, too.

As we shared the message of godly families, we noticed our own marriage continued to improve markedly. We were so much better at dealing with conflict; home was now an uplifting, encouraging haven, and we both felt secure and loved. Maybe this was part of God's plan for raising us up to be the FamilyLife directors. Hearing the message over and over, then sharing it and thinking "we've got a long way to go" caused us to really examine ourselves and strive for excellence in our own marriage. Sometimes I would be presenting a message of God's plan for marriage and think, "Oh, I thought I understood this, but NOW I understand it!" Key principles took on a deeper meaning for us each time we presented the message to other people.

At the time, we never realised how the principles that we were teaching and putting into practice for ourselves were providing the firm foundation we needed as we were headed toward our first major obstacle together.

chapter four

brushing against death

On December 26, 1998, I awoke uncharacteristically early at about
5:00am feeling refreshed and energised despite a late night and a typically
full Christmas of family festivities. The house was quiet, with Nikki still
sleeping soundly beside me. She needed all the sleep she could get—rarely
did the kids allow her the luxury of a sleep-in past 7:00. It wouldn't be
long, I thought to myself, before they would be older, and a good night's
sleep wouldn't be so rare. Just a couple more years.

Lying peacefully in bed, reflecting on the joy of Christmas, the great
time the kiddies had and how good they'd been amidst all the excitement,
my mind flickered then to Christmas morning. I had risen early for the
fourth time that week to go jogging around the Panmure Basin.

The double circuit of six kilometers had taken me the usual fifty minutes, not fast by any means, but boy it made me feel great. The morning had been warm and crisp. I was comfortable ambling along, in a mix between a power walk and a jog, at an even pace. No rush. Not like in the old days, when I felt like I always had to break a record or something. No, this had been quite different—cruising really, breathing in the clean air and the beauty of the new day. I felt in pretty good shape for my age.

Deciding to wait another hour until 6.00, I snuggled down, lightly stroking the muscles in my thighs with a kind of therapeutic stroke, as if to feel the progress I was making with my early morning jogs. Up and down. Suddenly my hands stopped. What was that? A lump? My heart began to beat faster as I felt the hard plum-size mass in my right groin.

"Uh oh," I said out loud. "Oh no. This can't be good."

Nikki was awake by then. She rolled over to look at me. "What is it?"

"I'm not sure, honey," I said. "I found a lump."

I knew the lump shouldn't be there, and I vaguely wondered whether it could be a kind of hernia-thing from the recent exercise routine. But deep down I knew otherwise, and I had a feeling it meant bad news.

I got up, made a cup of tea, and tried not to think about it. It was Boxing Day, and finding a doctor would be nearly impossible. I made up my mind to just try to put it out of mind as much as I could and wait until the next day to get it examined. My hand kept wanting to go to it, to feel the lump. It was quite large really, very hard, but it didn't hurt at all. I finally told myself that I would just get it taken care of and hope it didn't mess up our holiday plans.

Drinking my tea, I realised how much I was looking forward to this holiday. We sure needed one. It had been a tough, challenging year. Nikki and the kids hadn't had more than a weekend away in years. It was hard to say when was the last time we'd had a good bit of time away as family. The year before, we'd had all the drama of building and moving into a new home, so we'd decided to stay home for Christmas to work around the house. Apart from a weekend at Onemana Beach in September, we hadn't had any relaxing time away, either as a family or as a couple.

"Great management, Andy," I thought to myself. "And here you are director of FamilyLife. Good priorities, buddy!"

But this year, it was all planned. First we would have the annual weekend training event for our national volunteers and their families at the Sport n' Spa in Rotorua, then a week-long holiday just for our family. It was going to be excellent: Tash could go horseback riding, we could go hiking together, take the kayaks out, soak in hot pools, and just spend time with one another. Nikki would finally have a break. Then we'd return home with plenty of vacation days left to build a tree hut, turn the shed into a playhouse, and build a cover for the bikes. "Yep, that'll be choice," I couldn't help thinking, "as long as nothing bad happens."

Cancer itself wasn't entirely new to me. I had been on immune-suppressant drugs for several years to keep my body from attacking my kidney transplant. The problem was that these drugs also made me very susceptible to skin cancer, so I developed little spots all over my arms, legs, chest, and back that had to be cut out every month. One plastic surgeon bragged to me that I had helped him set a personal record by excising twenty-two skin lesions in one session. I remember counting over two hundred stitches and feeling like a pin-cushion afterwards. I had to get skin grafts from my thighs to help cover the holes. It was painful, but I had still felt well throughout it all. But this lump was different; this could be much more serious, and I knew it.

With all the doctors on holiday, I decided to ask my brother Jonathan what he thought. He was a veterinarian, and just happened to be home on leave from his practice in the U.K. "A vet is better than nothing," I reasoned.

Jonathan's prognosis was obvious by the look on his face. "Not good," he said. "You need a fine needle aspiration done now." Trying to make light of the situation, he added, "Try and stay off your hooves."

The next few days were a whirlwind of doctor appointments, biopsies, and five days of waiting and worrying about the results. When we finally got the results back, our fears were confirmed: the mass was a cancerous, fast-acting tumour. We needed to find a surgeon quickly.

A day before the surgery, the oncologist spoke to me and Nikki. "I don't like the looks of things," he said. "I think before we do this operation, you ought to get your affairs in order, just in case. You never know how things are going to turn out. Get your will sorted out, that kind of thing."

Get my affairs in order? Gulp.

It's a strange feeling to spend a day wondering if you're at the end of your life. My sister was fantastic and took the children off our hands for the day, and Nikki and I spent a very memorable day together. A heavy sadness hung between us as if we were on the precipice of saying out loud that this could be the end. We realised that all we'd come to gain— our great marriage, our three children, our ministry—could be lost. But instead, we focused on positive things like our special memories together rather than allowing self-pity or anxiety to ruin our beautiful day. The joy of reminiscing with Nikki and thinking about the wonderful life we'd had together seemed to chase away many of the doubts and fears and gave us an indescribable, wonderful feeling.

It was a beautiful summer's day. The sun was warm, and a fresh breeze was blowing in from the ocean. I had an odd kind of feeling: on one hand, I felt on top of the world, yet on the other hand, a heavy cloud seemed to hang overhead. We went roller-blading around Mission Bay hand-in-hand like lovers and stopped at a quaint restaurant for brunch. I remember feeling overwhelmed with love and thankfulness. I held her hand across the table and just looked into her eyes, feeling such a powerful love for her, and a gratefulness for the years God had given us together. Her hand felt small inside of mine. I realised that I wasn't afraid of death, but I did worry about what Nikki's life would be like without me. And I worried about Natasha, Olivia, and Ben growing up without a father.

"I love you, Nikki," I said, realising afresh just how much I really meant it. "You're such an amazing wife and mother. My life means so much more because of you. I'm so glad you married me."

I think that day had a profound impact on our marriage. Nikki and I know the truth of the cliché that life is short. Anything can happen at any time to change our whole world. We can't waste our time arguing or taking each other for granted. Every moment we have together is precious, a gift.

Nikki was so strong for me, so encouraging and supportive. "No matter what happens, we'll get through this. God's in control," Nikki reminded me.

She not only had to be strong for me, but for the children as well. Natasha, the oldest, was six and old enough to understand what was happening. Nikki tried to take her mind off of everything by helping her bake a cake while I was having my operation. At one point, Nikki leaned over to get some sugar and realised Natasha was crying quietly.

"What's wrong?" she asked her.

Natasha said, "I'm afraid that Daddy's going to die. Can you tell me that Daddy's not going to die?"

Nikki told me later that she was thinking, "Oh Lord, this is too hard. How can I tell my child something like this when I don't know what the future holds?" But then Romans 8:28 in Scripture came to her mind: "And we know that all things work together for good to those who love God, to those who are the called according to His purpose."

So she looked at Natasha and said, "Honey, I do not know what the future holds. I would love to be able to tell you that Daddy's going to be fine, that he's not going to die. But I can't tell you that because I don't know." She continued, "But God does say in the Bible that whatever happens He will look after us. The outcome may not be what you desire, it might be a hard journey, but God promises that you will be okay. God tells us we don't have to worry about tomorrow. You can trust Him."

I was so grateful for Nikki throughout the whole ordeal. She was so confident of God's faithfulness and was such an encouragement to me and the children. I don't know how I would have made it without her. Our children's faith really grew as well, as they faced the possibility of losing their dad and having to trust God for whatever outcome. It was a moment that caused them to place their dependency on God rather than on their parents.

I didn't die, of course, but the operation was terrible. In a sense, it was a success. The doctors felt fairly confident that they had removed all of the cancer by taking out as many as thirteen lymph nodes. I woke up in extreme pain, feeling as if my insides had been completely removed.

"How are you feeling?" Nikki asked me as soon as she could see me after surgery.

"Terrible," I grunted.

The incision didn't look quite right either. It leaked continually and eventually became infected. I couldn't walk for days, and the infection slowed my recovery time significantly. Needless to say, our vacation plans were thrown out the window. I spent weeks in the hospital healing from the surgery and the infection while Nikki juggled the responsibilities of taking care of the children, the house, and making sure she still had time to visit and encourage me at the hospital each day.

The oncologist visited me in the hospital a few days after the surgery and told us, "We do think the surgery went well, but the cancer had spread much further than we'd hoped. I still don't like your chances, so I'll tell you what: go do radiotherapy for about six weeks just to make sure. Because if this comes back, there is nothing more we can do for you."

So every day for six weeks, I went to the hospital for radiotherapy. Each day I spent up to two hours in the waiting room, then half an hour waiting for the doctors to attach all kinds of little applicators to my legs. The radiotherapy itself only took about thirty seconds. But Nikki and I knew it was worth it if it would ultimately save my life. We couldn't risk the cancer coming back.

Meanwhile, I was also going in for my regular renal checkups. The doctors had taken me off my immune-suppressant drugs so my body could fight the cancer, but it was causing my blood tests to come back worse and worse. I was in danger of losing my transplant. It was an impossible decision to have to make: Did I want to risk the cancer coming back, or did I want to lose my kidney? Neither, obviously.

I could see that if my transplant was going to fail, I had a narrow window of opportunity to do something I'd wanted to do while I was still able.

FamilyLife was thriving at this point. We were now running ten conferences a year all around New Zealand. Our volunteer team was growing, and another couple, Robin and Jill Rangeley, had just applied to join our full-time team. Actually, Jill had been amazing during the surgery, calling on me at home every day to help keep the ministry ticking along. With the ministry expanding so quickly, I was desperately in need of some inspiration and direction from our parent organization in the United States.

"I think we should go to Little Rock now while we still have a chance, before things get worse," I told Nikki once I had recovered enough from my surgery to consider travelling.

"I agree," she said.

We knew it might be our last and only chance to visit the FamilyLife headquarters in the States and meet Dennis Rainey.

Finally, in April of 1999, when I was feeling fairly well and confident about my recovery and had completed all of my radiotherapy sessions, we boarded a twelve-hour flight to the States. We were so excited about getting to meet the people we seemed to know so well from the conference video. Little did we know, another major hurdle was coming our way.

Unfortunately, I picked up a cold during the flight. We had a short layover in Dallas before we would make it to Little Rock. Nikki noticed that I was quiet and sluggish.

"Are you feeling okay, Andy?" she asked me. "You look kind of pale."

"I'm not sure," I replied. "I might be coming down with something. I have a terrible sore throat and congestion. I think I've just got a cold."

We were lugging our suitcases around the massive airport trying to figure out where we needed to go. I felt very weak; just lifting my luggage was a real effort. Time was running out before we needed to catch our next flight, and we suddenly realised we were on the opposite side of the airport from where we needed to be.

"Andy, we've got to go fast! Our plane leaves in about five minutes." Nikki helped steady me and took as many of the bags as she could manage, then led us onto the train that would take us to the correct gate. We dashed onto the plane just in time. I couldn't stop coughing, and I continued to go downhill from there as we flew the short distance between Dallas and Little Rock.

Nikki was concerned, but there was nothing she could do to help. My symptoms became worse and worse throughout the flight, so that by the time we finally landed in Little Rock, I was drained of energy and felt very ill. All I wanted to do was lie down and let my body get well, but we had three weeks of important back-to-back meetings scheduled.

We decided to go see a doctor first thing and, by God's grace, actually managed to get in touch with a Kiwi doctor, Mark Matthews, who was training in Little Rock. I can't tell you how comforting it was to connect with this guy who was outstanding in his quick grasp of our unique situation and his personal concern and care for me. He was incredible. I'm thankful for him to this day as my situation could have turned out so much worse without his help.

"Looks like you have pneumonia," he said. He was also aware of my transplant and that the cancer and my immune system might be causing complications. He took a blood test and, sure enough, it didn't look good. My body was rejecting the kidney.

"Now, this does not mean that this is the end of your kidney," Dr Matthews said, "but I do think it would be wise for you to do a couple of dialysis sessions while you're here just to keep you going, to give your body that extra boost."

"Oh, no," I thought, as the reality of actually losing my kidney became clear.

I agreed with Dr. Matthews that dialysis was probably the best thing to do. But I couldn't help feeling apprehensive, remembering the strain it had put on my first marriage. I had hoped Nikki would never have to deal with the pressure of dialysis, and now here we were in another country, and she was suddenly having to learn what it was all about. As Dr Matthews hooked me up to the machine, I said a silent prayer asking God to give me and Nikki the strength to get through whatever was coming. When the dialysis session was over, apart from the massive headache, I was surprised at the difference it had made.

"Wow—I feel all squeaky clean," I told Nikki. Of course, that only proved to me that my kidney had not been properly cleaning the toxins from my blood—not a good sign.

We tried to make the most of the trip in spite of my recovering from pneumonia and worrying about my kidney. I felt inspired just walking into the huge FamilyLife headquarters of over 200 staff. We did get to meet with everyone we had wanted to see, including Dennis Rainey, president of FamilyLife, and of course our dear friends Bob and Kathy Helvey, who invited us to stay at their home.

Everyone was so nice, giving us Kiwis such a warm and hospitable time, that we felt like royalty. They really gave us the red-carpet treatment. The design department provided us with disks of photographic resources; they loaded our arms with materials of every

kind; and we got to see firsthand their incredible vision for "I Still Do"—
a stadium event for 16,000 people. We also got to attend a live Weekend
to Remember (not on video), and also had the chance to experience
their parenting conference and new seminar called Understanding One
Another. Each event was superb and professional. On the last day, we
met Drew and Kit Coons, a couple who immediately understood our
unique needs for New Zealand. We began making plans to try to get
them to come down under to help out with our ministry.

In spite of all the memorable experiences, I was quite unwell the
whole time. I'm sure Kathy thought I was going to die on her couch, the
way I was coughing so much. Nikki helped me get around and stepped
up to keep the meetings going. I was thankful for the leadership and
initiative she showed.

I relied on Nikki a lot during the trip. And I knew that with my
transplant failing, I might have to rely on Nikki more than I was used to
from that point on. Doubt began to creep into my mind. "This is the kind
of thing that ruined your first marriage, Andy," I thought to myself.

Nikki and I were grateful for the time at FamilyLife, U.S. We learnt so
much about the ministry and were inspired and refreshed in our vision
for FamilyLife in New Zealand. At the same time, though, we realised
that the trip and pneumonia were probably speeding up the process of
losing my kidney.

We weren't blind to what was going on. We knew my transplant would eventually fail. How much time we had left, we didn't know. But we knew our lives were going to change drastically very soon. I felt confident in Nikki's love and commitment to me, but I could also see the potential for the situation to have a negative effect on our family.

Just two months after we returned home from our trip to the States, I went back on dialysis three days a week for six hours at a time. This was new territory for Nikki. And finding a way to keep it from affecting my family was going to be new territory for me, too.

back to the machine

"I've decided I'm going to do dialysis at the hospital instead of at home," I told Nikki one evening. "I don't want dialysis to mess up our marriage and family." We had been home from Little Rock only a couple of months, and it was very clear to us that I would have to do regular dialysis once again. Remembering the effects that dialysis had on my first marriage, I didn't want Nikki to have any responsibility in it. Dialysing at the hospital seemed to be the best solution for her, if not for me.

"No way!" Nikki said. "You need to do it at home. We'll never see you otherwise—you'll be spending all your free time at the hospital."

The next few days, I kept going back and forth in my mind on my decision whether or not to dialyse at the hospital. With Nikki's persuasion, I was glad to decide to give home dialysis a try—it really would be so much more convenient and flexible.

"But I want to do it all myself," I cautioned her. "I don't want you to help me get set up, put in the needles, or anything. I don't want it to be a burden on anyone at all."

"Okay," Nikki agreed. "If that's the way you want it, that's fine with me. We'll do whatever you think is best."

I had to go in for retraining because it had been ten years since I'd done dialysis. Nikki had to come into the hospital with me for some training, too, because I could only do home dialysis as long as there was someone else there with me who knew what to do in case of an emergency. Although Nikki learnt the basics, we agreed that she wouldn't do any of it unless there really was an emergency.

I remember looking around the dialysis ward and thinking, "Wow, all of these people are so courageous, and the world doesn't even know it." There's a lot of bravery in what they do every day. I knew I was going to have to summon the courage within myself to prepare for what was coming.

I was dreading having to put the needles in my arm again. That feeling of apprehension never goes away. I felt nervous remembering the pain of needling and the constant worry that something could go wrong, like my fistula packing up. Fortunately, my fistula—the access for my needles—was still operative after all these years. Dialysis hadn't changed much in the ten years since I'd had my transplant. It wasn't too difficult to relearn, but I was constantly on edge for the first couple of months.

Training was supposed to take six weeks, but I didn't want to be away from work that long. There was so much going on. We had added four more conference venues, expanding into Wellington, Invercargill, Rotorua, and even Pakistan! We had been asked to go up there to run a conference for expatriate missionary couples to help strengthen their marriages as they served in the field a long way from home. So Robin and Jill were making plans to head off there.

"I'll do the training in two weeks," I told the doctors, who I think were a bit annoyed with me. I was always hassling them to let me get going sooner than they thought I was ready. "Sorry, I just can't be off work that long." I trained for two weeks and then jumped back into my normal routine of full-time work with dialysis in the evenings three nights a week.

Dialysis was a huge change for the whole family. The children had never seen me dialyse, and just the machine itself can be intimidating, not to mention the needles sticking into my arm and the blood pumping into the unit. Even though I'd done it ten years earlier, it was a big adjustment for me, too. At times I felt very stressed and took out my frustration on my family in subtle ways.

"Kids, be quiet!" I yelled. "I've got to put these needles in, and I need silence!" They would look up at me with big eyes, surprised at the tone of frustration in my voice. Other times, if anything went wrong with the machine I would get upset, cursing it and so much wanting to kick it because of the inconvenience and stress of it all. Then I would hear the children crying and running down the hallway away from me. I felt terrible about my behaviour and lack of self-control.

"Maybe I should do this at the hospital," I told Nikki. "I don't know if this is working."

"We're all still adjusting," she said. "Give it a little time."

One time something went seriously wrong with the machine when I was in the middle of dialysis. Somehow, due to a faulty cap, the plastic kidney burst open at the top, causing blood to spurt up the wall. I panicked. No one was around to help, and I was physically tied to the machine by the needles. I needed to get a spare kidney from my garage and switch it with the broken one, but I had never been trained to do that. I didn't have a clue how to fix it. I was scared and worried about all the blood loss.

By the time Nikki and the kids came home, the situation was a little more under control (meaning blood wasn't squirting out the kidney and up the wall anymore), but I was still confused and panicking. I was yelling at the machine, clenching my fists with needles still in my arm, and doing a good job of once again frightening the children.

Nikki sent the kids to a neighbour's house and helped me get everything cleaned up. I even managed to replace the kidney on the machine. But my nerves were shot—I really had been quite frightened. Still, I felt ashamed for the way I reacted.

"I don't like it when you get frustrated and you lose it," Nikki said quietly. "I know you're worried. I understand that. It's a difficult situation when you know that if something goes terribly wrong, you could die. I can't imagine how hard it is, and you're doing so well. But it's scary when you lose it.

"I'm sorry," I said. "I know I shouldn't behave like that. I'll go to the hospital to do it. It'll be better for everyone."

"No, that's not what I'm saying. I don't want you to go to the hospital. Stay home. But please try and be more aware of us around you, okay? That's all I'm asking."

Sometimes it was difficult to keep from feeling anxious when things went wrong on the machine. Every month the kidney society sent us a newsletter, and on the back page was a list of the dialysis patients who had died that month. It made for sobering reading. I was very aware that while the machine kept me alive, the whole dialysis process placed added pressure on my heart, and life was uncertain. Although I wasn't afraid of death, I certainly didn't want to die yet and leave Nikki and the kids all alone. My worries seemed to intensify my frustration with the machine.

Apart from the dangers of dialysis, there were many times I had to miss special events—the kids' concerts or FamilyLife meetings because of a problem with the machine. Every time I got the machine serviced, my entire routine went out the window for at least a week as I waited for the machine to be repaired while dialysing at the centre during the day. During times when I had something very important planned, I would find myself begging the machine, "Please don't break down tonight. Not tonight!" Nikki would often pray with me and for me when I felt discouraged.

In time, as I got my confidence back, things did begin to get a little better, and so did I, although I still had moments when it was difficult to control myself. One time Ben came home in the evening, a happy boy excited to see his dad, and he jumped on my lap while I was on the machine. In doing so, he accidentally put his hand on the needles in my arm and pushed them straight through the back of my vein. Blood came gushing out from the needle sites, and a huge hematoma the size of an orange quickly appeared as pain shot through my arm. I picked the boy up with one arm and practically chucked him across the room as I pulled the needles out.

"Ben, you idiot! You've got to be more careful!" I said, gritting my teeth through the pain.

"I'm sorry," he said, trembling and worried as he watched me try to control the bleeding.

"It's okay. Just... be more careful." I closed my eyes and tried to hold myself together. The agony was nearly unbearable.

It wasn't until the next morning that I had a chance to put things right with Ben. I got down on bended knee in front of him and apologised.

"I'm sorry for yelling at you last night, buddy. I know you were just trying to be nice and you didn't mean to hurt me. I'm all okay now. Would you please forgive me?" He did without hesitation, and we enjoyed a nice hug together.

That experience, as unpleasant as it was, gave me the opportunity to teach my son. We might not be perfect, and we don't always do things right, but it's an important lesson our children learn when they see us admit our mistakes.

Although I was getting better about controlling my emotions, dialysis was still having a larger effect on my family than I would have liked. They adjusted well, but I hated having to put them through the trouble of it all.

The daily drudgery of it was wearying. The toxins in my blood made my skin itchy, and many nights I had trouble sleeping. Also, I had to control my diet strictly, which meant that many of my favorite foods—including most fruits—were permanently off the menu.

I was allowed to drink only 600 milliliters of fluid a day, which amounted to about three cups. I spread these throughout the day so that I chose to have a cup of tea at 10.00am, 2.00pm, and 6.00pm. During the time in between, I was often thirsty. My throat dried out and I counted down the hours and minutes until I could have a drink again. Day after day of a never-ending thirst made me realise how good I'd had it when I was able to drink as much as I wanted without giving it a second thought.

Another challenge for the family was that I could never be away from the machine for more than a few days, so we could go on holidays for only three days at most, unless I made arrangements at a hospital or dialysis unit. Never could I have the choice to just take a break from dialysing. If I felt unwell, I still had to do it. When I had my wisdom teeth removed, I still had to do it. On a stormy night with thunder and lightening, when there was a big threat of a power cut, I still had to do it. After running a Weekend to Remember marriage conference and finally returning home exhausted at midnight, I still had to do it.

One night, Nikki and I were spending some time together, just sitting outside and talking. But I was feeling a bit down.

"I'm sorry, honey," I told her. "Because you married me, your life is so hard. My health makes things really difficult for you."

"No, you've got that wrong," Nikki said. "My life is so good *because* of you. You're the best decision I ever made."

My love and thankfulness for Nikki nearly overwhelmed me. It was amazing the ability she had to give me power and impetus when I needed it, even when I didn't deserve it. A woman is powerful in the words she can speak into her man and get him through the roughest day. I had plenty of rough days, but with Nikki beside me cheering me on, those dark moments seemed almost trivial. I resolved to continue working on my frustration and make the best of the situation—I at least owed that much to her.

As I became more accustomed to being on the machine and saw how my family drew together to get through the difficult times, it even dawned on me just how grateful I was for it in some ways as it caused me to really appreciate what was truly important in life. It would have been great to be free of the machine, but perhaps it wasn't the solution I was seeking. In those moments of weakness and hardships, there was so much to be grateful for—supportive friends and family, Nikki's unconditional love, God's provision for us in every area of our lives, the strong family relationship we all shared. It caused us to really suck the honey out of the day. I reminded myself that people who have good health and all the trimmings of a successful life don't necessarily have happy lives at home.

Deep down, I still battled discouragement daily, though. Along with dialysis, the pressures of operating a full-time ministry in the midst of all of these changes was starting to overwhelm me. I firmly believed in my heart that God had given me a mission and a vision, but being chained to this machine took away my freedom to do that. The needs in New Zealand were so great with families falling apart, but I felt so restricted. It reminded me of the apostle Paul in the Bible when he was in prison. He was so passionate about serving God and felt frustrated that he was locked away, unable to do what he really wanted to do. Yet he said he had learnt the art of contentment and still sang praises to God. I was still trying to do that.

I felt sure that God wasn't telling us to step down from the ministry, but how long would I be able to keep up with this? I often didn't finish dialysing until 1.00am–2.00am. Then crawling out of bed the next morning always took a colossal effort. If I was honest, I had to admit that I felt lousy most days, and I didn't know how I could keep the weariness from affecting my work. One thing I was determined about was that I didn't want my fatigue to adversely affect those around me. I had to be strong.

I thought back to a conversation I'd had with Nikki on the flight home from Little Rock, when I had realised dialysis was imminent.

"Nikki, do you think this is God saying that He doesn't want us to be involved with FamilyLife anymore?" I had asked her. "I mean, look at these obstacles. Maybe we're not supposed to be doing this."

"I really don't know," Nikki said.

But then, Nikki came across 1 Corinthians 7:20, which said, "Each one should remain in the situation which he was in when God called him." When she shared it with me, it was exactly the verse I needed at that time. It was as if God was saying to me, "My calling for you is still the same. Nothing has changed. You may have doubts in yourself, so work through me instead." It was a tremendous encouragement to receive affirmation that I should continue doing what I was passionate about, knowing that as long as I was obeying God, He would continue to use me in the ministry and give me the strength to persevere.

I knew I would just need to keep reminding myself of His promises on the days when I felt discouraged.

As dialysis became more of a normal routine for me, I got better at taking the bad with the good. Dialysis was continually a burden, but I could see the ways that it was a bit of a blessing in disguise. Even though I could never learn to fully embrace the machine, I learnt to accept it. After all, without it I would have died, so in a way I could even be thankful for it. My faith grew as I had to rely on God more and more. The ordeal actually made our family appreciate each other in a deeper way, because we were aware that there were no guarantees on how long we would all be together.

Meanwhile, I had plenty of work to do that helped take my mind off my health. At FamilyLife, we were fully aware that the video conference we were using was approaching its expiration date, having been filmed in 1986. While the messages were still life-changing and very relevant, the clothing styles were looking old-fashioned. It was time to update it. The only trouble was, the video conference was not seen as a popular medium by FamilyLife headquarters. In most countries around the world, the FamilyLife Conference was delivered live. However, our staff was not yet trained to a point where doing a quality live presentation was possible. And the video had proved so popular with all who experienced it; it had even shaped our own lives and marriages so dramatically that we felt we had to stay with this strategy for another five years until we felt we were ready to do the messages ourselves. The video conference was an instant means to reach people all around New Zealand.

But if the ministry in New Zealand was to remain credible, we had to get permission from headquarters to re-film the conference. I waited with baited breath as our request was considered by the leadership team in Little Rock.

I got the phone call I was waiting for from Dennis Rainey himself. "Andy, the team has granted you the permission you need, with three conditions. You use our film crew here so we can be assured of its quality, and you pay for it yourselves. Finally, you have to agree to this by January 20."

"That's fantastic news, Dennis. We'll do it," I said without hesitation. I had thirty days to find the money—US$90,000—but we had to do it!

I held an initial meeting and called a large group of ministry supporters together to outline our plans for this new conference. I was incredibly enthusiastic and passionate because I could see just how fantastic it would be and how many marriages would be strengthened. The video conference was so portable—an instant ministry!

But by the somber reception, I quickly noted that my words were falling on worried ears. With an exchange rate of 40c in the dollar, we were going to have to raise almost NZ$200,000!

There were many hard questions: Why so much? Why can't you take your own film crew? Where will you find that kind of money? But despite it all I still felt confident that it was a "must do", and that we could do it. To me it was a no-brainer, even if most of the people in that board room didn't feel the same. Then, towards the end of the meeting, one man did the one thing that I needed to put legs to the idea. He pulled out his cheque book and wrote a cheque for $10,000. Only $190,000 to go!

While fundraising continued, I began to make arrangements for the filming. There was a huge amount to organise. We chose the same awesome speakers that we were used to, Dennis and Barbara Rainey and Bob Horner, whom we had to brief on speaking in a way so that their messages were aimed at New Zealanders—a difficult assignment in front of an American audience. They were speaking to an audience of nine hundred couples in Roanoke, West Virginia.

I had the privilege of flying to the United States to oversee the production, obviously needing to arrange a number of dialysis sessions while I was there. It was a big moment, as we had one shot at this with it being a live event, and we had to get it right. The film production crew was top notch. We had about six cameras and a huge production studio with numerous monitors and staff to ensure everything went according to plan. Which it did.

On arriving back in New Zealand we continued to raise funds while the sixteen hours of raw footage went into post-production. Of course, eventually all the money came in, not before I'd almost sent us and our entire parent ministry, Campus Crusade for Christ New Zealand, under financially—but it did come in. The new video conference arrived in flash digital format on DVD (no longer video cassettes) and it has been used extensively ever since to touch lives and transform marriages and families—not only here in New Zealand, but around the Pacific and in Singapore, too. To date more than 16,000 people have experienced this conference. What a tremendous encouragement this bright spot of our lives was to me and Nikki.

President,
Orakei Tennis Club

Receiving a Gold Design Award
(centre) while at Insight
Communications. Mike Tisdall, the
Managing Director, on the right.

Wedding Day 20 January 1990

After winning a Downhill Slalom Race
in Hopfgarten, Austria, during honeymoon.

Proud moment: New Zealand team flag-bearer at the 7th World Transplant Games, in Singapore 1989. New Zealand came 16th overall.

First New Zealand Team, World Transplant Games Singapore, 1989.

The 4 x 200m Relay Tea

After winning the Bronze Medal in the Senior Men's Tennis Doubles at 1997 World Transplant Games in Sydney.

Athletes competing at the World Transplant Games have one thing in common; they have all had a successful organ transplant. By taking part they aim to raise global awareness of the importance of organ donation.

There's no greater gift than the gift of life and World Transplant Games athletes from so many countries worldwide are living proof of that.

With FamilyLife Founder and President, Dennis Rainey, during the FamilyLife Conference in Roanoke West Virginia, 2000. (Andy was there to oversee production of the filming.)

Live on-air on their regular weekly radio programme 'Family Matters' on Radio Rhema.

Staff Training in Sydney.

Celebrating 10 years of ministry in NZ with special guests Bob & Jan Horner and Bob & Kathy Helvey and the NZ Staff and volunteers in Taupo 2001.

Presenting yet another Weekend to Remember Marriage Conference at the Waipuna Hotel Auckland.

Project time.

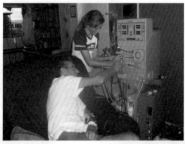

Dad and Natasha at age 12

Olivia helping her dad set up the dialysis machine which he needs to connect to three nights a week for 5-6 hours

Dad and Olivia at age 5

Being his own Family LifeGuard at Opoutere Beach

Dad and Ben at age 6

chapter six

disaster strikes

One of the biggest misconceptions we can make is when we think that life will one day get better. We think, "One day when... " and by doing so, we miss out on being content with how things are. Nikki and I were about to learn this lesson quite keenly, as though dialysis, a failed kidney transplant, and cancer weren't enough to deal with.

After several years of being on dialysis, I began to develop a strange and severe itch under my skin. It's common for dialysis patients to experience a chronic itchiness, but this itch was much worse than anything else I had experienced.

No matter how much I scratched, the itch wouldn't go away. It was in my blood. I scratched and scratched at my back until it bled. I could hardly concentrate at work because all I could think about was getting rid of this horrible, irritating, persistent itch.

I would stand against a carpeted wall during meetings and rub my back against it for whatever small amount of relief it would grant me. My team at work would joke about it, but it was privately driving me crazy. It got so bad that I couldn't even sleep at night—the itch kept me awake. I would go for long walks outside in the middle of the night with my shirt off just to feel the cool night air against my back—the only thing that seemed to provide relief.

It got worse as the weeks went by. "I don't know how much longer I can take this," I told Nikki. "There's got to be something wrong here." I remembered feeling itchy the first time I went on dialysis years before, but never to the extreme that I was experiencing at this point.

Nikki felt helpless as she saw my spirits rapidly drop. She woke up in the middle of the night one night to hear me yelling, "I just want to die! Please, Lord. Take this away from me!"

"Lord, why does this have to be so hard?" she prayed. "Not only is he on dialysis, but now he's got this itch and he can't relax enough to fall asleep. It's too much for him."

Every morning I would go to work, eyes red from having no sleep. I was in absolute misery. I went for three months with virtually no sleep and a constant, terrible itch. Nikki hated to see me in such a state.

"I'm going crazy," I told her. "The idea of heaven seems very appealing right now."

"Please don't say that," she pleaded.

I knew she hated to hear me talking like that, but I was so plagued that it seemed only death would bring relief. I never dreamed I'd be a person who even thought about suicide.

We finally saw a doctor about it and found out the problem: my parathyroid glands were overproducing calcium—a fairly common occurrence for dialysis patients. It was this overproduction of calcium in my blood that was causing the itch. The doctors examined me and determined that they would need to remove the parathyroid glands from my neck.

I'd once seen a man in the dialysis unit soon after he'd been operated on for the same condition in the local hospital—it looked like they'd removed his head and put it back together again. It did not look good. We knew it would be a bit rough, but anything would be better than this itch that was just too distressing.

I wanted to find an expert in the field and get the best possible job done, so we spared no expense and found a private doctor to do the surgery rather than go through the typical public system.

"What's the operation like?" I asked him.

"Well, the parathyroids are pretty tricky to find," he said.

That wasn't what I wanted to hear. "How much of a risk is it?" I asked him.

"Oh, not much. No, I can do it. Don't worry. It's just a bit tricky."

He explained that he would need to cut across my throat, then he would take out nearly all of the parathyroids, leaving just one. "You'll need me to leave at least one gland just in case you ever have another transplant," he explained to me. "You could manage without them, but they are actually useful things to have."

I agreed to everything, desperate to get rid of the itch. I worried that my neck might look disfigured afterwards, but there was no way I could continue living this way. The surgery was my only hope.

We asked friends and family to pray for me before I went into surgery. We didn't expect it to be a major operation, and we had a top surgeon working on me. With my health history, though, we knew nothing was ever straightforward.

I knew that with the operation, I wouldn't be able to dialyse for at least three days. So right before I went into surgery, I dialysed for a little longer than I normally would have. The machine took about three kilos of fluid out of me, leaving my body dehydrated and my blood pressure very low—around 90 over 60. It didn't help that when I arrived at the clinic, everything seemed to be in chaos. The nurses were running around frantically, and no one seemed to have time to make sure my body was adequately prepared for surgery. I entered surgery in a disorganised rush for some reason, and the next thing I remembered was waking up and feeling very strange.

Meanwhile, Nikki got a call at home from the surgeon, who said, "Everything has gone great. No problems." Nikki hung up, relieved. It was late Friday night by then, so she made plans to come and see me the next morning.

Saturday morning, on her way to the hospital, Nikki received another call from the surgeon. "Nikki, I just need to let you know—nothing to be too alarmed about—but I just need to tell you that Andy suffered a post-operative stroke."

"Is he okay?" Nikki asked.

"It really wasn't major," he explained. "As Andy was waking up, his body had a stroke. It affected his arm a little bit, but he'll be fine."

"Oh, okay," Nikki said, not feeling too troubled. She didn't even really know what a stroke was anyway.

By the time she got to the hospital, I was in intensive care. The doctors came in and began tapping my feet and asking if I could feel it. I couldn't. I could tell something was seriously wrong with my body.

Nikki came in, and I could see the shock on her face. The entire left side of my face had completely dropped, and I was paralysed down the left side of my body. I couldn't speak, so I just looked at Nikki and cried.

The doctors came up to Nikki and explained that I had suffered a second, more severe stroke during her drive to the hospital. "We're going to do some brain scans and different exercises to try to figure out exactly what went wrong and how serious this is," they told her.

After about three hours of tests and scans, they were able to conclude that a blood clot in my brain during the operation had caused the stroke. "What we don't know is how much you'll gain back. It's important that you gain it back quickly because the sooner you're able to walk, talk, and use your arm again, the more likely you are to retain your abilities."

My mind could hardly process everything that was happening. What was this going to mean for me and Nikki, and for our kids? What would this mean for the ministry? I felt so frightened and vulnerable. I didn't want Nikki to leave my side—I needed her comfort.

After she had spent all day in the hospital with me, the nurses encouraged her to go home. "You need to rest," they said. One of my nurses was a committed Christian and part-time pastor. He told Nikki to call him at any time of the night if she needed to check on me.

"I'm praying for him," he told Nikki.

"Thank you," Nikki said. "That means so much to us right now."

The next weeks were some of the darkest moments of my life. As horrible as kidney failure had been, nothing could have prepared me for dealing with this. I felt like a vegetable—all I could do was cry (an after-effect of the stroke, I was to find out later). I had completely lost all of my independence. I still needed to dialyse, but I couldn't do it for myself.

The nurses had to hook me up to a dialysis machine and put the needles in for me. I had no control over my arm, so it flopped around while they tried to get me set up. One time the needles popped out and blood began rushing out of my arm, but I couldn't feel it. Blood gushed out until I finally looked down and noticed the growing red pool under my chair.

The doctors were uncertain about how much normal use of my body I would gain back. We began a grueling eight-week period of rehab. My world consisted of rehab and dialysis, then more rehab and dialysis. I hated to have to be away from home for so long, but Nikki was amazing. She was there to support me and encourage me every day. Her steadfast love is what got me through those weeks of depression as I struggled to do simple tasks like walk and speak. She even slept on an armchair in my room at night as often as she could.

Progress for me was painfully slow in the first week of rehab, although I did learn to walk and talk again—not perfectly, but it was a start. However, I still had problems with my right arm and had no fine motor skills in my left hand—it was just a clenched-up club. I was dependent on the hospital staff for so much—bathing, getting dressed, tying my shoelaces. You never think about how difficult it is to do the buttons on your shirt with one hand until you try it. My reliance on other people felt like a prison. And I missed my children so much.

I went to two rehab sessions every day, and each day I was asked to do the impossible. I tried walking in a straight line, going up and down stairs, and lifting small dumbbells to strengthen my arms. I read books aloud, trying to retrain my mouth to form the words properly. My balance was gone, so as I walked around the ward, more often than not I banged into walls and doors and often fell on the floor. Nikki was there to cheer me on and encourage me to keep going when I felt like giving up. It was so frustrating to be given a seemingly simple task to do and not be able to do it.

For several days in a row, the physiotherapist sat me down at a table and spread some beads out in front of me; he then asked me to pick them up one by one and put them in a jar. I concentrated so hard on those beads, willing my damaged hand to move towards them and for my fingers to close around a single bead. I just couldn't do it—my movements were awkward and clumsy. The delicate beads were too small for me to grasp.

"You're doing a great job," Nikki said. "You've really come so far."

The truth was, I felt like a three-year-old, and a huge burden on her. I felt so guilty for putting her through all of this, but I needed her.

One day, I felt particularly down. "I just want to get out of here," I told Nikki.

She thought for a moment. "I might be able to arrange that," she said. "At least for the afternoon."

I perked up. About an hour later, I was riding in the car with Nikki, on the way to the Panmure Basin—my favourite running spot. "I don't think I'll be able to do any running today," I said sarcastically. My left leg still wasn't working quite right. But it felt amazing just to be outside in the real world again. Nikki walked beside me and kept me steady as I hobbled around for a couple of hours. By the time we got back to the hospital, I felt refreshed. "Thank you for that; it was a gift just to be outside," I told Nikki.

"It was so good to see you walking out there again," she said.

Nikki's enthusiasm was contagious. It dawned on me that of all the other patients in rehab alongside me, very few of them had regular visitors. Nikki was there with me every day to keep me going. When I felt frustrated by all the things I couldn't do, she reminded me of what I could do. I needed every drop of encouragement she gave me. I had never really understood depression before—I thought if someone just made up their mind to "snap out of it" they could. I was finding it wasn't so simple as that.

Nikki sat with me every day for hours, even though I was often grumpy, disappointed, and depressed. Every time I saw her walk into my room, my face lit up and I felt more and more determined to work hard so I could go home and be with her and the kids as soon as possible.

Christmas was fast approaching, and I began to wish I could do something for the kids, knowing the last several weeks had been pretty lousy for them. They'd been shuffled around to different friends and relatives so that Nikki could be with me in the hospital; so not only were they worried about my stroke, but they were also having to be apart from us a good bit of the time. But with our ministry salary, I didn't think there was much we could do to give them a special Christmas.

I had coffee with Nikki in the hospital café and explained what I was thinking. "If only we had an extra $500 to get us through this next period," I said. So we did what we always did and prayed about it together.

When Nikki returned home that night, she found a letter in the mailbox from our friend and supporter Murray. "I've enclosed a cheque for $1,000," the letter said. "I want you to have a great Christmas. Go out and spoil the kids." When Nikki told me, I was so overwhelmed that I wept with appreciation.

One day around that time, my brother Chris flew in from Melbourne to make himself available to me and the family. He took me for a jaunt in the wheelchair to places we weren't meant to go, and I was glad for the sense of freedom and adventure he gave me that day. Later he went to my home and helped my son build a rabbit hutch. They were simple things, but they really touched me.

In spite of the bright spots, I privately continued to battle depression and discouragement. My time in the hospital was like a test for our marriage. I was incapable of giving anything to Nikki—no passion or real companionship. I was absorbing all of the love Nikki could give me without being able to give her anything in return. She extended grace to me in an incredible way by continuing to show me love when all I could give back was a temper and a bit of depression and negativity. It was a long journey working through those emotions, but without Nikki I would have fallen apart.

I also had to work through some questions with God. We'd had a lot of people praying for me before the surgery that it would go well, and instead it turned out much worse. Where were the answered prayers? Why could other people go through this same type of operation with no problem? Did God still have a plan for me, or was this it? FamilyLife was still going strong; we were now hosting sixteen conferences a year.

Another couple, Markus and Bronwyn Hasler, had joined our staff team. Drew and Kit Coons had responded to our invitation and had come out from the States for two years to help us develop a one-day marriage seminar and to train us as speakers. What chance was there now of me doing any speaking? Besides, the ministry seemed to be getting on just fine without me. Maybe they didn't need me anymore. What then?

As a man, sitting in the dark on my own, I felt I'd had much of my manhood stripped away. My body was pretty useless; I had no great career to rely on, no incredible house or material wealth to feel good about. Pretty soon I had to find my self-esteem in all that was left: who I was in God's eyes.

I stayed up at night reading my Bible, searching for guidance and wanting to know what all of this meant for my future or for me as a person. I found a verse that I felt was very clearly from God. Isaiah 45:3 (NLT) said, "And I will give you treasures hidden in the darkness—secret riches. I will do this so you may know that I am the LORD." I was in a dark time of my life, but I was reminded that God would give me something to hold on to.

It was as if God was saying, "Get your chin up off the floor. There are people in this place much worse off than you are. I'm at work right now, right here in this dark place. You don't have to be at FamilyLife to serve me. Look around—there are people in great need all around you. You can experience life with me here, too."

God speaks to you when you're well, but His promises seem to shout to you in the midst of your darkness and pain, and you can hear it deep in your heart. God's presence felt so real to me, and with so little left to cling to, my faith strengthened and grew. I began to develop a huge appreciation for what I did have. I could see people all around who were worse off physically and who didn't have the kind of support that I did. As I started thinking about all of this, a thought hit me: I could go and visit every person in the ward and do what I could to cheer them up. It was like a personal challenge I made to myself. Something I could *do* rather than mope around all day.

"Is that what you want me to do, God?" I asked. "Is that what I'm here for?"

Immediately, I began having doubts. I could hardly even walk—how was I going to be of any use to anyone? But I couldn't ignore the challenge. With God's help, I could do it.

chapter seven

a new perspective

Once I'd given myself a personal challenge to visit every single person in the ward, it was easy to know where to begin: Jonathan was in the bed right next to me in the same room. We'd already had a chat or two, but this was to be different—I wanted to spend time really focusing on him and getting to know who he was.

Jonathan was an enjoyable conversationalist. He was happy to tell me about his interests and goals—at least what they used to be. He was seventeen and a musician. He played guitar and wrote songs for a local band, and he'd had dreams of becoming a professional someday. He had grown up a normal kid, but then tragedy struck only a few nights earlier; he got up in the middle of the night to go to the bathroom, and his legs wouldn't work—he had been struck down by muscular dystrophy, a degeneration of the skeletal muscles that control movement.

Jonathan was very obviously discouraged about the direction of his life. "I've lost everything," he confided in me. He shook his head and looked down glumly. "There's no cure for muscular dystrophy. I can forget about music and a career. There's nothing for me."

I felt so sorry for him. At least I'd already experienced so much of life; at seventeen, Jonathan was really just a kid. We were both still coming to terms with what had happened, feeling very insecure and unsure of our direction. I began spending some time with him over the next couple of days, learning about his background and personality. Our conversations in the beginning revolved mostly around rehab and how long it would be before we could leave. Jonathan had plenty of family sitting with him during the day, but after they'd leave I think he appreciated having someone there who could really identify with what he was going through. I sympathised with Jonathan's depression, but I also had confidence that although his life as he knew it may have been over, there was still so much more he could do despite this major setback.

Trying not to make him feel uncomfortable, I searched for the right words to say. "God really helps me get through my dark times," I told Jonathan. "I still feel down sometimes, but He helps me to keep going."

"Oh, yeah?" Jonathan said, polite but not exactly enthusiastic.

"Sure," I said. "I believe God gives me the strength to remain optimistic. I get great encouragement and hope from reading His Word."

I showed him my copy of a daily quiet time book called *Word for Today* and handed it to him. "This has helped me a lot," I told him. "It's inspirational. I'd like you to have it."

"Thanks," he said, still unsure. I didn't know if he would ever give it a second thought, but I hoped that the biblical truths would encourage him and give him a new perspective. Sometimes we would just have random chats. Other times, we watched movies together.

"What are you watching?" I asked one day as I wheeled over to his side of the room.

"*Gladiator*," he said. "Have you seen it yet?"

"Nope."

He motioned for me to join him, so I did. There was something comforting for both of us, I think, in just having someone nearby who was facing many of the same challenges and doubts.

I don't think anything I did had a noticeable impact on him, but I hope that he was at least uplifted in some way. I caught him reading the daily devotional on a few occasions, so perhaps God used a verse or two to speak to his heart. Before long, Jonathan was moved to a specialised MD facility. It was time for me to meet some of the others.

In a room a few doors down was an Indian man who always wore a turban and caftan. He had suffered a severe stroke—his second or third, actually—and was unable to walk or talk. I don't know much about his story because he couldn't speak much English, but that didn't stop me from spending time with him. I smiled at him and sat down beside him, just to give him some company because no one else was there with him and he seemed very depressed.

I sat on the edge of his bed for about fifteen minutes, talking all the while and not knowing whether he understood much of what I was saying. He didn't seem to ever have any visitors and he had a very sad face. I poured cups of tea for him, wishing I could do more.

Another gentleman down the hall was a sixty-eight-year-old former businessman. Both of his legs had been amputated because of gangrene, but he was still very vibrant and positive.

He proudly told me about his business. "I used to own a big delivery company with all these trucks," he told me. "Built it all up from scratch." He told me the name of his company. "You ever heard of it?"

It sounded familiar. "I think so," I said.

"Oh, well. Anyway, we made a fortune." He laughed heartily. "Those were the days... but mind you, I've still got some good days to come."

I was in awe of this man who was such a breath of fresh air, especially considering what he was going through. He sure helped put my troubles in perspective. Here was this old guy who had lost both his legs, but was still so sprightly and independent. I paid him several visits over the next couple of days and became quite friendly with him. He was fun to be with; we laughed about all kinds of things, and it turned out that *he* cheered *me* up!

I was sitting with him one day when a very important delivery arrived for him—his new prosthetic legs.

"Are you ready to go for a walk?" the prosthetic specialist asked him.

"Sure, let's do it!" he said. "At last I get to walk again! Now, how do I get these things on?"

"We'll get them on you in no time." The specialist looked over at me. "Andy, I might need you to help support his other side. Are you up to it?"

"Sure!" I said. To be honest, I was still pretty dodgy on my own legs, but I couldn't pass up the opportunity to help my friend try out his new legs.

I watched as he slipped his chopped off legs out from under the sheets and the specialist put his new legs gently into place. You would have thought we were in a shoe shop trying out new shoes, the way he took it all in stride. After a few minutes, he was ready to go walking.

"Let me hold onto your shoulder," he told me as he gradually inched his way toward the edge of his bed. Slowly he stood up, a bit wobbly, and began moving one leg forward. "These are great!" he said, delighted. I felt so privileged to be there at that moment. It was fantastic seeing his enthusiasm. Just then he lost his balance and had to sit back down to keep himself from falling.

"Good try," I said. "It'll take some time to get used to them."

He grinned. "I'll be running all over this place in no time, you just watch!"

"I believe it."

True to his word, as soon as the specialist was satisfied that the prosthetic legs fit correctly, the old guy was out of there. He had a life to live and didn't want to waste any more time. I felt so inspired by him. I thought I was going around trying to encourage others, but God used this experience in a subtle way to lift my eyes off my troubles and my fears about the future and put them in perspective. I still had my legs—they weren't working like they used to, but I could walk! Feeling refreshed by the vigor I had seen in this man, I told myself that I would be running again in three months.

The more time I spent with my fellow patients, the more we began to develop a spirit of camaraderie, and the more I realised I was actually enjoying myself. In rehab, whenever one of us made a major breakthrough or hit a milestone, the therapist would announce it to everyone out loud so that we could all cheer.

"Scott just took his first steps without any assistance!"

"Mary was able to balance for five minutes!"

In rehab, we had a communal dining area where we would all eat breakfast together. The nurses explained that the idea was for us to be rehabilitated back into the community again. It struck me as a bit funny—

we were like something out of that movie *One Flew Over the Cuckoo's Nest*: a whole table full of people with brain damage, useless limbs, and various oddities associated with our particular cases.

My first introduction to the breakfast table was rather depressing. No one had much to say; plus it was incredibly frustrating as most of us were using one hand, trying to butter our toast or open milk containers. I especially hated those stupid single-serve containers of butter and marmalade with peel-off foil lids. They were impossible to open with one hand. We also had big aluminum teapots full of tea that were very difficult to lift and pour with one hand.

After a day or two, I became uncomfortable with the quiet and the introverted way we were helping ourselves. It seemed a bit unreal—strangers eating together in silence, independent of each other.

"Anyone for tea?" I asked, carrying the teapot around. "Milk? Sugar? One lump or two?" I picked up the sugar bowl and held it out.

"This is a rehab ward," a nurse interrupted. "We're trying to help you get ready to go back into the community. The very reason you have these challenges is so that you'll find a way to help yourself. If you help each other, it will short-circuit what we're trying to do for you."

I understood what she meant, but it seemed ridiculous that we couldn't help each other. It was more likely that I would go hungry than get the toast to stop sliding around long enough to put butter on it.

One day, after a frustrating fourth or fifth attempt to open a jar of jam, I decided to try my methods again. I looked around to make sure there was no nurse present, then turned to the guy sitting next to me—another stroke patient.

"Hey, mate—would you please hold this jar for me with one hand so I can open it? How about you hold your toast and I'll butter it for you, then I'll hold my toast and you can butter mine?"

"Great idea," he said eagerly.

The idea caught on fast as it made things a whole lot easier. Pretty soon everyone at the table was pouring tea for each other and helping their friends open the containers of milk and butter. The nurses noticed what was going on and ran over to put a stop to it.

"We want you to be able to do these things on your own!" they insisted. "So that you can be independent."

"But we're just being a community," I reasoned. "We're helping each other."

Now that we knew how much easier it was to help each other than to try to do it ourselves, we weren't keen to go back to the old way. When the nurses weren't looking, patients around the table would hurriedly butter one another's toast. Watching the things that took place over breakfast was quite a riot. I'm sure the nurses knew what was going on; they just chose to turn a blind eye.

Meanwhile, I continued going from room to room until I had met and talked to every person there. Because Nikki had been so amazing at coming in for hours every day and instrumental in comforting and encouraging me, I knew the importance of having someone around if just for comfort or support. Nikki had been that person for me, and now I felt I could be that person for others.

Nikki was still coming to see me every day to encourage me. "Knowing what some of the other patients are going through makes me thankful for what I have," I told her one day. "I see people who are dealing with major, life-altering situations and struggles that will never fully go away, and I've just got a paralysed arm and stuff. It seems small in comparison."

I felt that because I had made the effort to get to know the others and cheer them up, my troubles had been put into perspective. I even found I was enjoying myself and making friends. Being there didn't seem like a prison anymore. I had found my treasures in the darkness that God had spoken of in Isaiah.

When I was released, Nikki had to be briefed on what we would need to do when I got home. She told me later that one of the nurses came up to her and said, "I wish we had more patients like him. It would make such a difference to our job." Wow—that felt good to hear.

When I finally was able to go home to be with my family, I realised that most of my depression had lifted in the time that I had taken the focus off myself and concentrated on helping others. Besides, there were plenty of people helping us, too: providing meals, taking care of or children, mowing our lawn—all kinds of things to help us cope. I even had my own personal physiotherapist, as our good friend Bronwyn Collins made the long trip to our house three times a week to take me through a number of exercises.

I knew there were challenges still ahead of me as I would have to re-adjust at home, but I had the promise of Isaiah 41:10 to sustain me: "So do not fear, for I am with you; do not be dismayed, for I am your God. I will strengthen you and help you; I will uphold you with my righteous right hand."

chapter eight

living with purpose

Rehab was all about equipping me to cope with real life, but then I returned home from the hospital and got ready to go back to work. I was immediately discouraged by how long everything took—simple tasks such as tying my shoelaces and putting on a shirt and tie. From the first day at home onward, I never wore a tie again and began to buy shirts without buttons. Nikki had to help me get ready for work every morning, and everything took twice as long as it did before the stroke. It was nearly impossible to open the toothpaste and get it onto my toothbrush or squirt shaving foam into my palm one-handed. I guess in the hospital it never really troubled me, as I had all day to get ready, but now I had to worry about getting to work on time. I knew that some of my abilities would return with practice, but the process seemed painfully slow.

Some skills I would never gain back. It pained me to think that although I used to be able to give Nikki a fantastic back massage, I just wouldn't have the fine motor ability to do it anymore. I couldn't even hold her hand. Nikki often had to cut my meat even when we went out to a restaurant. I couldn't play basketball or netball with the kids or enjoy a game of tennis with Nikki. There were so many things I desired to do but couldn't. I used to type eighty words a minute, but couldn't do touch-finger typing anymore. Still, I was determined to persevere.

Eight weeks after the stroke, I was still walking quite slowly. "It takes me two-and-a-half hours to walk three kilometers," I told Nikki.

"But at least you're walking," she reminded me. "And you're much steadier on your feet than you used to be." I thought then of my good friend Jack Govind, who broke his back skiing and could no longer stand up. "I'm pretty fortunate, really," I thought, knowing just how much Jack would have loved to take just a few steps.

On grocery days, I would help Nikki carry the shopping in from the car. On one occasion, I arrived in the kitchen only to look down and find the bag no longer in my hand. I had inadvertently dropped it outside somewhere without even realising it.

As the weeks went by, I began to notice incremental improvement in the use of my arms and legs. One day I was outside helping Nikki hang up the washing (hanging about one item to her ten), and I said, "You know, darling, I'm just enjoying being able to do something as simple as pegging clothes on the washing line. I always used to think it was a chore—I'll never take it for granted again." Using my left hand, I picked up a peg and clipped it onto the line as a demonstration. I couldn't explain how good it felt just to be out in the sunshine doing something so seemingly insignificant.

"Well, aren't you clever!" Nikki said, equally excited.

Clip, clip, clip. Never had I so much enjoyed helping with laundry.

During my recovery time, my dad had come over nearly every week to tie up the rubbish and take it out. I didn't want to have to rely on him for that anymore, so I focused on learning how to do it myself. With some practice, I finally got it.

One morning I tied up the rubbish and carried it out. The sun was out again and I felt on top of the world as I said to myself, "Look, I can take out my own rubbish bag, and it feels great!"

As I went inside afterwards, I said to Nikki and the kids, "I just want to tell you how good I felt taking the rubbish out." Every little step that allowed me to gain back my independence was like a celebration to me, because each little task took so long to master.

I had to take a special driving exam to prove that I was still capable of being on the road after having a stroke. I took numerous simulated driving tests in front of a big screen designed to monitor my response and reaction times—incredibly difficult tests that even able-bodied people might have difficulty passing. Two people in the car monitored every move I made (one-handed I might add). I had to follow their directions on a two-hour practical driving test, naming every warning sign that I saw on the way. Thankfully, I was granted my license once again. It was quite a milestone as it would make getting to and from work much easier, not having to rely on someone to take me in and pick me up every day. One step closer to a normal life.

One night the whole family was sitting down to dinner, eating, and having ordinary conversation. I had a special fork made specifically for stroke victims—a normal fork was too small for me to hold. For four weeks I had tried and tried to use a knife and fork and to attempt to put food to my mouth, but hadn't been able to. Finally, on this occasion, I managed to cut off a slice of meat and lift the fork all the way and take a bite, concentrating so much that I was not aware anyone was paying attention. Suddenly, there was an eruption of applause as the kids rose to their feet in celebration around the table.

"Well done, Dad!" they yelled.

It's funny the kinds of things that I appreciated after my stroke—the fact that I could take out the rubbish, for example, or lift my fork, or a million other little things. I began to see great value in the tasks that my hands could do. I even managed to shave my two-and-a-half-hour walk down to nineteen minutes for the same distance. Rather than focusing on all of the things I couldn't do anymore, I developed a great thankfulness for my capabilities. I had an entirely new perspective that spilled over into every area of my life.

Even my family picked up on this concept. We saw each moment together as a gift, with no future guarantees. If you brush past death enough times, you get to a point where you don't take many things for granted, especially family.

We found unique ways to celebrate our family and the time we had together. One of our favourite traditions was what we called the "Beaut Bray Award". The award was actually a bronze medal that I had won at the World Transplant Games in Australia a few years earlier, but we used it as our family award. Once a week we all sat down at the dinner table together and began the ceremony of awarding the medal to someone who had done something to deserve it. We didn't give the award for performances, academic achievements, or other things one might typically applaud. Rather, it was for good decisions they'd made or character qualities that we noticed God was cultivating in their hearts.

"Who deserves the award this week?" Nikki and I would ask.

We let everyone say who they thought deserved it most and why. Then Nikki and I would have the presentation of the medal, and we all sang a song we made up to the tune of the national anthem. It was all a bit corny for an observer, but it was a tremendous encouragement to the kids as we praised them for the types of things that are important to God. It's easy to catch your kids doing something wrong; we wanted to catch our kids doing something right. And it was fun!

"The world is a negative place out there," we told our kids. "We want our home to be a very uplifting and encouraging environment; we want to speak encouraging words to one another."

Another way we encouraged our children was by creating a "love book" for each child. In these books we could write encouraging notes to them, telling them how grateful we were for them and how much we appreciated and loved them: "Olivia, I want to tell you again just how wonderful you are, how much I love you. You have an amazing gift of compassion; you seem to know exactly what a person needs and you just go out and do it. You've demonstrated that to me several times this week. I love you." The kids got involved as well by writing special notes to each other.

One thing we would not tolerate was disharmony in our home. Everyone's days are numbered, but we had felt the pressure of that reality a little too closely to allow backbiting and bitterness to get a foothold in our lives. I knew, because of the many years I had been on dialysis, that I was living on borrowed time.

About five months after my stroke, Nikki and I had the opportunity to speak at a one-day marriage seminar in Hamilton. I had made a lot of improvement in those five months, but could I really speak in front of an audience?

"I don't know if I'm ready for it," I confided in Nikki. "But I'm determined to try."

I began reading books out loud to the kids at bedtime to prepare myself. My words still seemed thick and slurred, and occasionally my mouth looked a bit strange, but I was getting better. Having a goal in mind caused me to work harder than before so I could be ready in time.

On the day of the seminar, just before it was to begin, doubts began growing in my mind. Was it ridiculous to think I could really do this? Nikki could tell I felt a bit anxious.

After taking time to pray with Nikki, I took a deep breath and walked out on the stage, nervously surveying the crowd of about one hundred. While I'm sure they would have noticed, I felt it would be best to explain my difficulties right from the start so that in case they detected me struggling, they wouldn't have to wonder what was wrong.

Nikki and I introduced ourselves. I said, "I recently had a stroke. So I apologise if I'm difficult to understand. This is the first time I've spoken at a seminar since it happened." I also briefly explained that stroke victims sometimes have trouble controlling their emotions.

Nikki and I took turns presenting the material that day, and the seminar was fantastic. The audience seemed interested and enthusiastic; they laughed at our jokes and worked hard on the couples projects between sessions. I had some difficulties, of course, crying each time I told a moving story, which made them all start crying, too. Still, I felt so encouraged knowing that I could still do it. I don't think the audience really even noticed my struggle.

I soon began to notice that God was using my experiences to minister to others, not just in spite of my trials but actually *because* of them. I spoke at a Building Your Mate's Self-Esteem Conference in Auckland one weekend, and the first night I introduced the audience to my family by showing pictures on a large screen of me and Nikki with the kids. As the weekend progressed, I not only presented the marriage material, but I also shared some of our personal struggles as we had dealt with my health issues through the years. After the conference, a man came up to me.

"When I saw the photograph of your picture-perfect family, I thought there's no way you could ever understand me and my problems," he said. "I thought you must have everything under control, and you couldn't possibly relate to my situation. But after listening to you, I said to myself what have I got to complain about? What right do I have to be unhappy?" He continued, "Even with all of that, you still have a strong family. I can do that, too."

Another time, I shared my testimony in a church and mentioned my experiences with dialysis, cancer, and the stroke and how God helped me to work through those tough times. A young lady walked up to the stage afterwards and said to me, "Thank you for that. I just found out last week that I'm diabetic. The news crushed me. I was on the worship team, really involved with my church, but I had chucked everything away. I was angry with God. But your story has really encouraged me. I'm going to start singing again next Sunday." We developed a deep compassion for people struggling with hard times, having gone through so many ourselves.

One night a young couple, who were friends of ours, rang us because they were having marriage trouble. "We really need to come for counselling," they said. "It's urgent!"

"Nikki's out this evening, and I have to dialyse, but if you think you can handle that, you're welcome to come. I'll be glad to see if I can offer some suggestions." I was used to having meetings at my home while I dialysed, so it wasn't a big deal.

"Thank you," they said. "We really need to come." About half an hour later, they showed up. They let themselves in and made themselves a drink, as I was already on the machine, then sat down on the couch across the room from me.

"So, tell me what's going on," I said.

We had barely gotten started when the power suddenly went off and threw us into darkness. The machine began alarming, telling me that it had stopped working.

"Do you need to come off the machine?"

"Well, that's one option, but since I can't see anything, that would be rather difficult," I explained.

"What else can you do?" they asked.

"I'll have to manually pump the blood to keep it moving so that it doesn't clot," I said. "And I'll just hope the power comes back on soon. But I'll need your help."

"Sure, what can we do?"

I tried to stay calm as I instructed them on where to find a torch, matches, candles, and a bucket. "Let's get these candles going, then go fill the bucket with warm water," I said.

While she stood holding a torch and lighting candles, the husband filled the bucket. "Now reach down beside my chair and put my blood lines in the water to keep the blood warm. That will keep it from freezing since the heater has shut down on the machine."

I continued pumping by hand as five minutes went by, then ten minutes. "I think I need to come off the machine," I said. "It doesn't look like the power is going to come back on anytime soon." So I gave them instructions for one to hold the torch and the other to continue hand pumping the blood while I went through the process of disengaging from the machine, getting my blood back, and removing the needles. Just as I got off and felt safe again, Nikki rushed through the door and the power came back on.

"Are you okay?" Nikki asked.

"I'm fine," I said. "I had a lot of help."

I apologised to our friends and thanked them profusely. "Now, where were we?" I asked. "How can we help you?"

"No, forget it," they said. "I don't think our problems are going to be much of an issue anymore. Tonight has sure helped us put everything in perspective. Thanks!" And with that, they were gone.

I've done dialysis now for a total of nineteen years. At three days a week, for six hours at a time, that's more than 17,000 hours of being on the machine. Whenever I started to feel bogged down in the daily grind of dialysis and just doing what I had to do to survive, or when I felt discouraged by the after-effects of the stroke, such as the difficulty of doing something simple like holding a shopping bag with my bad arm, I would remind myself of the great things God was still doing in and through me.

It greatly encouraged me that God was using me despite my weaknesses and limitations and we were witnessing God still changing lives. It reminded me that God does all the work, we're just involved in the process. And we saw how God used my disability as an encouragement for so many others in difficult circumstances. "I think I've learnt to accept that life is now different," I explained to Nikki one evening as we walked around the block together. "God has allowed dialysis and a stroke to be a part of my life, and I need to be content with where I am right now in my new circumstances. In a funny sort of way, I'm kind of thankful because it's made me appreciate at a deeper level so much that I used to take for granted."

"Well, that's great, but I'm not sure I want us to learn any new lessons for quite awhile," Nikki replied truthfully.

"And, honey, there's another thing I've realised," I continued. "Often we long for things to get better and, we say, 'one day when' or 'once this has happened, then we'll'. And instead of things getting better, they can actually get a darn sight worse. Like me. I just wanted anything to take my itch away, and this is what happened. I must admit, though, it's so nice to be able to relax at last without that constant irritation. But the point is, we shouldn't always look to the future for things to get better because they might not."

I can relate with the apostle Paul when he said that he had been given a "thorn in the flesh". Although we never learn what that particular "thorn" was that he pleaded with God to remove, we do get to read God's answer and Paul's acceptance in 2 Corinthians 12:9-10:

But He said to me, "My grace is sufficient for you, for my power is made perfect in weakness." Therefore I will boast all the more gladly about my weaknesses, so that Christ's power may rest on me. That is why, for Christ's sake, I delight in weaknesses, in insults, in hardships, in persecutions, in difficulties. For when I am weak, then I am strong.

I also think about how the apostle Paul was a man on mission, a driver, and how being in jail must have been so incredibly frustrating for him when he preferred to be out travelling and sharing the gospel. Yet being in prison gave him time that he probably wouldn't have given himself to write parts of the Bible that are so important to us today. So, as difficult as it must have been for Paul, there was a purpose and a plan in all of that.

Paul and I are somewhat alike in that we're both task-oriented people with big goals and plans. I'm afraid that without my health problems, I might have wasted my life by working and climbing the corporate ladder. It's made me know where my priorities should be, that's for sure.

My struggles taught me the art of contentment and how to make the most of the best and the least of the worst. It's not the life I would have chosen for myself, but I finally reached a point where I could chime in with the famous hymn and sing, "It is well with my soul."

chapter nine

a stronger marriage

Many times I've wondered what I would have done all these years if I hadn't had Nikki. Her love and faithfulness have truly been a glimpse of heaven. Although I wouldn't have chosen to have my kidneys fail, get cancer, and have a stroke, I have to admit that all of those things have brought us into a deeper relationship that I wouldn't trade for anything.

Nikki has seen me at my lowest points and has given me a reason to keep going when I wanted to just give up. She's been my comforter and companion and has loved me at moments when I wasn't lovable.

We saw our marriage strengthen over the years, not only through trials and our need to rely on each other for support, but also through the daily decisions we made to protect, preserve, and improve our marriage.

One morning I got out of bed feeling really grumpy. I'd had a bad dialysis session the night before. I hadn't started until late, so I'd been tired the whole time and had just wanted to go to sleep. Plus, the machine had acted a little funny, and I hadn't been able to dialyse for as long as I needed. I woke up feeling fed up with the machine and grouchy from a lack of rest. Unfortunately, I took out some of my frustrations on Nikki. After she had watched me storm around the house trying to get ready, she asked, "Do you need anything? Do you want some tea or something?"

"No," I said irritably. "I'm going to be late." I barely glanced at her as I continued gathering the things I would need for the day.

"Kids, pick up this stuff you left all over the floor!" I yelled, trying not to trip over stacks of books, shoes, and other odds and ends scattered across the living room. "I'm leaving," I told Nikki.

"Okay, well—have a good day," she said quietly.

It wasn't until I got to work that I calmed down enough to realise I hadn't treated Nikki the way I should. Upon opening my e-mail inbox, I noticed I had a new message from her. I sighed, expecting to see a note telling me that she didn't appreciate the way I had treated her or asking me to speak more kindly to the kids next time. Of course, that's what I deserved. Instead, the e-mail said:

> *I was just folding some wash and thinking about what an*
> *amazing hubby you are. I continue to admire the way you*

faithfully take the kiddies out for breakfast once a week—you

may wonder whether you're having an impact. Take it by faith,

you're having a huge impact, and you will only ever know it

when they are older and can tell you some of their treasured

memories. Being "up" for the family takes a great deal of effort—

thanks for striving to be the best you can be. I appreciate all

you do, the notes to us all, comments in their books, art classes,

keeping the home and garden neat and tidy, cleaning our cars,

reading to the kiddies when you're on the machine (I know you'd

rather crash, but you never say no), plus so much more. We

think you're terrific and we are blessed to have you as our family

leader, husband, and dad. Your loving honey...

I nearly bawled my eyes out. This e-mail wasn't what I deserved at all. I immediately called Nikki, apologised for my behaviour, and told her how grateful I was for her. Nikki truly demonstrated to me that day the power of giving a blessing for an insult, a principle we had taught before at our marriage conferences.

Nikki was also an excellent role model for the children in the ways she demonstrated love and acceptance when I didn't deserve it. For example, one summer we dropped Natasha off for a few days at a horse-riding camp called Sunshine Ranch. On the last day of camp, they had a show scheduled at 3.00 so that the parents could come see the things their kids had learnt. It was Natasha's first time there, and we knew it was very important to her that we be there for the show.

The day of the riding show, I got caught up in a heavy phone counselling problem at the office and lost track of time. When I realised I was late, I left in a rush and arrived home to see Nikki standing in the driveway with Ben and Olivia, ready to go. We had only fifteen minutes to make it all the way to Clevedon, a forty-minute drive.

"Hurry, let's all get in the car," I said. I could tell Nikki was upset, but she didn't say anything. I broke every traffic law in the book, trying to make it as quickly as possible.

"There are tons of kids there," I said, trying to reassure them, "And it only started at 3.00. I bet some of the younger classes will go first. It'll be fine. We'll get there in time."

Thanks to my driving, we made it to the ranch at about a quarter past three—only fifteen minutes late. We ran down to the corral where the show was going on. And there was Tash, sitting on her horse and looking great. We'd made it just in time! But then we watched as she rode out of the stadium and back down to the stables where the horses were kept. We had missed her after all.

Tash was pretty upset with me. She was crying and didn't want to speak to me or even look at me. Mr "FamilyLife" man had let his own child down badly. She had kept five photos in her camera especially for me to take of her riding around on her horse and going over the jumps. But of course, I wasn't there to take any photos, let alone see her. So she was fed up with her dad, and I knew I'd really blown it. It was my own fault—I left work too late.

Nikki was frustrated, too. She could have gone to the horse ranch without me and wouldn't have missed the show. But no, she waited for me without knowing whether we were going to make it in time. Even though she was upset as well, she took Natasha aside and said, "Honey, I'm so sorry we missed your show. I really am, and I know how disappointed you must be. Tash, Dad feels absolutely terrible about letting you down, and you can see he's pretty gutted. But it's too late to do anything about it now. You know it's not like him, so let's not give him a hard time. We need to forgive him and release him from feeling so badly."

Nikki gave me the freedom to fail and taught our kids an important lesson. We have a daily choice of whether we want to live in unhappiness and resentment, holding things against one another, or whether we want to live in grace and choose forgiveness and acceptance. It brings out the best in each of us and makes us strive not to make the same mistakes over and over.

We don't always handle things the way we should. That's why it's been important for us to also learn the biblical guidelines for resolving conflict and granting forgiveness. I remember one Saturday night Nikki and I had a big argument, and we hadn't quite gotten over it by the time we went to bed. The next morning, we woke up and began getting ready to go to church. I ended up saying something that morning that started the whole thing up again. By the time we got in the car to go to church, we weren't speaking to each other.

We went into church and just put on a mask for the time being, greeting our friends and pretending that everything was just fine. After church, while walking out to the car, we began snapping at each other again. We drove away, still arguing, caught in a downward spiral of trading insult for insult. Finally, I'd had enough.

I pulled the car off to the side of the road. "I'm outta here," I announced. "I can't take it anymore." I got out and began walking, leaving the car running with Nikki and the kids inside.

After a few minutes, I heard the car pull away from the shoulder. I glanced over to see Nikki driving away, headed for home. My kids were staring at me through the window, wondering if their dear old dad was ever to be seen again. Even as I walked away, I was thinking, "Andy, this is stupid. You're miles from home. What are you going to do now?" But I was still angry enough that I didn't really care.

After about two hours of walking, I was tired, hungry, and annoyed with myself for my behaviour. "I'm an idiot," I thought. "And now I have to go and tell Nikki I'm sorry and ask her to forgive me." But I was still quite far from home, and my pride didn't want me to admit that I had blown it. Just when I thought things couldn't get any worse, it began raining.

Finally, I made it to our doorstep and walked into the warm, dry comfort of home, looking like a drowned rat by that point. Nikki's face lit up as soon as I came in.

"I drove around looking for you," said Nikki, relieved to see me.

My pride seemed to melt away. "I'm so sorry," I told her. "I was really stupid. Can you forgive me?" It wasn't as hard to say those words as I had made myself believe it would be.

"Of course," she said. "I forgive you—and I'm sorry for the way I acted as well. But did you remember there's a couple coming here tonight for pre-marriage counselling?"

I had completely forgotten. Needless to say, I felt totally inadequate to give anyone pre-marriage counselling, considering the events of the day. Moments later, the couple showed up. "Hey, Andy, was that you we saw walking out there in the rain?" they asked, coming in and getting settled on our couch. "What were you doing out there?"

I looked over at Nikki, dreading having to tell the truth. To think I had been worried that apologising to Nikki would hurt my pride—this was much worse! But I had no choice. I explained the whole situation to them and even used it as an illustration on how not to let their pride keep them from saying the words "I'm sorry". The good thing was that we got better at seeking and granting forgiveness with more practice. We also got into the habit of having a weekly date night to discuss tough issues or simply to enjoy new ways of keeping our marriage fresh and strong.

We realised early on that many couples are missing out on the tremendous benefits of having a weekly date night. In fact, a lot of people don't even understand it. Nikki took Olivia to a netball game one evening, and towards the end of the game she turned to one of the other mums and said, "I've got to run. I've got a date night."

The woman looked at her, surprised, and said, "What? I thought you were married."

"I am," Nikki said.

"Well, who do you have a date night with?"

"My husband," she replied. "Andy and I have a date night once a week."

"Wow! What do you do on a date night?"

"Well, we really just get together and talk for a couple of hours. We don't go to the movies or a concert or anything and usually don't spend any money. Sometimes we walk along the beachfront or maybe just get a coffee at a café, and we talk about our relationship and our kids or we plan important things coming up in our lives so that we can stay connected and keep romance a priority."

"How cool is that!" the woman said, blown away. It had never occurred to her that married couples should continue to date and pursue one another.

We also used date night as a way to deal with disagreements. On days when we had an argument or began to sense some tension in the issues we were discussing, we would say, "Time out. Let's take a break from this and make plans to talk about this next week on our date night." By the time date night rolled around, we could discuss the issue free from the emotions that would have led us to get angry or upset the week before. It was a great way to take the pressure off each other by lovingly placing the issue on the table at a later time and figuring out together how we could come to a resolution.

We say to couples at our weekend FamilyLife Marriage Conferences, "Your spouse is God's perfect provision and gift for you." That is so true of Nikki. God knew just what I needed when he brought her into my life. Not many women could have put up with what she has with such grace and commitment to being a godly wife and mother.

Looking back on some of the hard times we went through together, particularly the stroke, I once asked Nikki, "How did we ever get through that?"

"I don't know," she said. "I guess we just bunkered down together, trusted God, and hung on for our lives. You and me against the world."

I'm still not sure how we managed to make it through to the other side, but I do know I couldn't have done it without Christ in my life or without Nikki. I've needed her for comfort, support, and encouragement.

I'm reminded of Ecclesiastes 4:9-10 that says, "Two are better than one, because they have a good return for their work: If one falls down, his friend can help him up." How many times have I fallen down and needed my best friend to help me up? More than I can count. I've dug into Christ for my self-esteem, significance, and security in the darkest of moments, and praised him through everything.

Not all of the things Nikki and I went through together were bad things—we have tons of good memories together with our children and of the wonderful ways God was working through FamilyLife. One year, we produced booklets of tips on things to do with your kids. They came with cassettes and were packaged colourfully and professionally. We sent them out to garages, supermarkets, workplaces—anywhere they might sell—and we went through 20,000 in three months. Men would call us up from the side of the road after listening to the tape in their cars and say, "I just want to tell you that this has really touched me. I was driving along and just started crying. What else can I do? I heard about your conferences—how can I go to one of those?" It was exciting to see the way God used something so simple to change people's hearts.

We also took a big leap of faith together when we raised the $200,000 needed for the new conference video project. It built our faith tremendously and was cause for a big celebration.

We were able to see the new video being used throughout New Zealand as a powerful tool as many people learnt about God's plan for marriage and families.

I think that circumstances like these wouldn't have been quite as significant without Nikki there beside me. We've needed each other not only in the bad times but in the good times as well. She's wept with me when I've wept and laughed with me when I've laughed. Those moments of laughter were treasures that went a long way in sustaining us through the times of darkness and tears.

chapter ten

jump in puddles

At one point I thought I had finished writing this book. I thought I had
gone through the worst of my struggles and had learnt all the lessons I
would need to learn. I was wrong.

The physical pain of my sickness has always been difficult. But
nothing could prepare me for the type of pain that came in the next
chapter of our lives.

On Tuesday, 15 April 2008, we were settled in for a typical weekday
night at home. I was on the kidney machine, as usual, while Nikki was
cooking dinner and the children were doing their homework. We weren't
a complete family as Natasha was away with her school at the Outdoor
Pursuits Centre (OPC), an adventure camp in the Tongariro National Park.

Over the weekend she'd been so excited about going, but she did
share one concern with us: "I'm scared about going canyoning, Dad.
I don't want to do it."

Listening to the heavy rain on our roof, and knowing there was a national storm warning in place, I reassured her by saying, "Honey, don't worry. You won't be going anywhere near a river in weather like this."

That's why we were flabbergasted to receive a phone call from our good friend Jo. "Did you just see the TV news?" she asked.

"No. What's happened?"

"Some children are lost on a river at the Outdoor Pursuits Centre. Isn't that where Natasha is?"

Thinking there might be more than one school at the camp, Nikki asked, "Do you know which school is involved?"

"No," Jo replied. "It was just a short news flash—that's all they said."

From that moment on, we intently focused on obtaining any little titbit of news that was available. We turned the TV on; I connected to the Internet on my laptop. Nikki rang the school a number of times, but was unable to get through.

Finally Nikki connected with Murray Burton, the school principal, about eight o'clock. Murray confirmed our worst fears. It was our school, and Natasha was one of the ones lost on the river.

We imagined the group of seven sitting on the banks of a river somewhere, freezing cold, in the dark, waiting to be found and rescued.

I quickly sent off e-mails and made a few short phone calls to close friends and family, briefly telling the situation and asking them to pray with us. Then I made a frantic call to OPC hoping to get information on the actual state of our children.

A lady named Jill answered. "I'm one of the parents of the missing children," I said. "Can you tell me what's going on, please?"

"I'm sorry, at this stage I can't," she said. "There's a cordon around the centre, and I can't tell you anything else at this point."

"We're coming down there," I said.

Jill replied, "I would recommend against that at this stage, sir, until we know more. May I suggest you contact the Taumaranui police. They might be able to help."

Quickly hanging up, I phoned the police station in Taumaranui. The man who answered was very official, as cops are, and simply asked for my name and number and promised to call me back once they knew anything.

I was still in the middle of dialysis, but I said to Nikki, "Let's go down there. As soon as I get off this stupid machine, we'll drive down."

She replied, "I'm going to the school to see what I can find out there." And she left. I felt as helpless as ever, connected to the machine, unable to comfort or hug her. I realised I was having difficulty breathing properly, and my chest felt tight. With nothing more to do but wait, I sent Natasha a short text message: "Tash, please let us know u r ok asap we r very scared and worried luv dad."

Over the next few hours, the living room began to fill up with family and friends who had come to sit with us and support us. Nikki returned a short time later, reporting that a prayer vigil had been set up at the school, but they still hadn't heard anything.

Just then, on my laptop, the Internet news flashed an announcement: "Four Dead in Canyoning Tragedy at OPC." I quickly shut my laptop almost as if trying to deny what I had just seen. I couldn't bring myself to tell anyone, least of all Nikki. As far as we were concerned, Natasha and the other children were just lost. Surely the media had it all wrong— surely someone would have told us already if this were true.

But deep down I had a premonition that we were facing a much bigger trial than we had ever imagined. I prayed quietly for Natasha. "Stay strong, darling— help is coming. Please God, take care of her. Keep her safe." I knew she was strong, a good swimmer. She spent hours boogie-boarding in huge waves each summer. She'd done a lot of outdoor activities. She was well equipped.

"She'll be alright," I said out loud, trying to instil confidence in myself as well as everyone else.

And then a TV news flash confirmed that at least four had died.

At that point, the whole room took on a different feeling. Nikki was frantic on the phone trying to find out any facts. Who? When? How? Is this true? Why haven't we been informed? What were they thinking to take them onto a river in weather like this?

But all the time, we continued reassuring each other that Natasha was still alright.

In a way it gave us hope that no one had phoned us.

Finally, I decided to come off the machine, even though I was about two hours early. I withdrew the needles and put the machine into rinse mode, and finally stood up to give Nikki a big hug.

"Shall we go down to OPC?" I asked. "She'll need us." But it was almost midnight, and we were uncertain what would be best.

I walked into the family room. Brad, our pastor, was there, along with many close friends and family. I suggested we all go into the lounge and pray together.

I hustled them into the lounge and asked everyone to stand in a big circle and hold hands while I prayed out loud. "Lord, we don't know what to say. We feel very helpless. Please keep Natasha safe. Give us wisdom on what to do next. Please bring her home safely. Be with her. Give her courage. Give us courage. Amen."

I phoned OPC and the Taumaranui police again, but this time I couldn't even get through. Then we heard on the news that one more had been found dead. We felt helpless and in shock—this couldn't be happening. With five dead, only two people were left unaccounted for. It had to be Natasha and her good friend Portia.

"She's alright," I kept saying, but my confidence was falling on deaf ears.

There was a dark, sombre mood in the house. I kept holding on and praying for the news I desperately needed to hear: that Natasha had been found, cold and upset, but alive and safe. But we were about to hear otherwise.

I'll let Ben's words, written later as part of a school work exercise, tell the story of what happened that night:

> I lay my tender red face down onto the seeping wet pillows; waiting, wondering in a mental cloud of darkness. Peering at the clock reading 16 April, 2:47am. I silently begged God to spare an awesome sister and mostly an amazing friend. Cries from the lounge made me spring to my feet. I steadily opened the door as light from the lounge crept into the sombre room. Through the diminutive space I wearily gazed across the lounge to see a mournful police officer grasping a police hat in his shaky hand. Surrounded by tearful bloodshot eyes.
>
> Just at a slight glance I knew! Suddenly I felt light-headed and confused; I felt like I was going to faint or completely lose it and pulverize everything in sight. But all I could do was flee, hide, and cry. Lying in bed unable to sleep, I concealed myself in the covers praying that this mournful night was just a horrible dream.

The police officer sat at the table. "Are you Andrew Bray, the father of Natasha Bray, sir?" he asked. "I'm sorry to have to report to you that your daughter has been confirmed dead from drowning."

The entire room erupted in a cacophony of tears and loud wailing, the likes of which I had never before experienced—it was like watching Middle Eastern people on the news after a bomb has just hit. I was in shock, but for some reason totally unemotional. I wasn't very aware of what was going on around me—I was only aware that because of the noise, I couldn't hear what the policeman was saying.

"Please, just be quiet for a minute."

The kind officer, through red, tear-stained eyes, continued to provide more information in his police jargon. He stayed about ten minutes, and then informed us that he must go and see another family.

The worst possible outcome had happened. We were in shock, absolutely devastated, unable to come to terms with what we'd just been told. My first thought was for Natasha, as I pictured her down in that cold, dark, unwelcoming river, without us there to help. And then deep down, this gut feeling of condemnation began to well up for the Adventure Centre, its management, and instructors, for taking my daughter into such a dangerous area. What were they thinking to go near a river in weather like this? That question continued to boil inside me.

Sleep for me was impossible.

The next day, we decided to attend the morning school assembly. We sat near the front of the school auditorium in an area reserved for parents. TV cameras and radio journalists stood nearby. The assembly was quiet, very sombre. Nikki and I seemed unable to look people in the eye. We hung onto each other, close to tears the entire time. It still felt so surreal, as if it weren't actually happening. We were not really aware of anyone else—not even the cameras that were pointed at us—but we knew we were being hugged by everyone around us.

The principal, Murray Burton, came to the front and prepared himself for the most difficult speech of his career. He quickly outlined the basics of the tragedy.

> *Six of our students—three girls and three boys—and a male teacher died yesterday after heavy rain swiftly turned a river the group was canyoning down in the Tongariro National Park into a torrent.*

He then spoke very slowly, pausing a second or two as he read out each name. The names seemed to echo around the two-levelled auditorium, and the list seemed to go on forever.

> *Yesterday we lost Portia McPhail ... Anthony Mulder ... Tom (Huan) Hsu ... Natasha Bray ... Tara Gregory ... and Floyd Fernandes. We also lost Mr McClean.*

As each person's name was read out loud, there was an audible gasp from the assembly, with much crying and sniffling as students heard who had died the previous night. Mr Burton continued:

If our faith means anything at all, it must mean everything now. Having said that, I have no answers, you have no answers, we have but miles of questions, and that is human. And students especially, I want you to ask as many questions as you want to ask; cry and grieve, talk and write poems. This process is long, but it's going to be good because we believe in God who created this world. He began it, He sustains it, and He will end it. He is a God worthy of your trust—He gave His own son. He alone knows how our families and you feel today. I refuse to stop trusting in Him—I can't work him out, and that's a good thing because He is God. Be angry; I don't mind if you're angry. Be angry at God—He can handle that— but keep trusting. We just need to stand shoulder to shoulder, side by side and work it through.

Following the assembly, which left Nikki and me with tear-stained faces after so much crying, we were led to the school library for a meeting with the police and the other families.

We introduced ourselves to each other and hugged one another with a unique understanding of the pain we each felt. Portia McPhail's mother, Nadia McPhail, said to us, "We are connected at the hip forever."

Danie Vermeulen, the chairman of the Board of Trustees of the school, introduced himself. He gave us a brief outline of how the school was planning to respond and how they wanted to help. The police then gave us a summary of the night's events regarding the search and recovery of our children, but without much detail, as they didn't yet have much to give us. We were advised that a number of investigations were being instigated, not only by the coroner, but by the Labour Department and an internal one by OPC.

We were then warned about the massive media contingent waiting outside. It was not just the Elim School in Auckland that had been plunged into mourning, but the entire nation had been shocked by the deaths. The media was hungry for a story.

"If you don't voluntarily offer them something, they will still need to get their story," the police told us. "They will climb walls or follow children home after school to get news."

After the meeting ended and the group disbanded, I felt a firm arm on my shoulder.

"You're needed," my good mate Brent said. "You need to sit next to Murray and speak to the media. We'll protect you. You have to do this."

And with that, I was hustled out of the library to a room packed with people. I took in the sea of microphones on long boom handles and cameras of all types with long telescopic lenses. At the front was a table at which Murray Burton and a few others were sitting and speaking.

It seemed as if I were led by bodyguards all around me like the US President as I was shown to a chair next to Murray. He turned briefly to acknowledge me, then continued describing the seven people lost.

And then one of the reporters asked me a question. Suddenly I felt the full focus of attention shift to me. I felt intimidated by the cameras pointed at me from every direction. And what could I say to even begin to describe what I was thinking and feeling?

"I'm a dad who's lost his eldest daughter, 16," I began. "These kids were remarkable young people; selfless, giving their lives to make a difference. They loved God, and they wanted to be part of making this world better. We've lost some amazing difference-makers, some role models. And my daughter was one of them. My wife and I had great dreams and expectations of how God might use her to make this a better world.

"These were kids of extraordinary character who set themselves aside to be involved in building up others who were struggling. So this is a real tragedy for New Zealand. Who knows what these kids might have gone on and done? And their standards were so high—I know this isn't a worldly way, but my daughter hadn't even kissed a guy. So they had those kinds of standards of excellence that are unusual in our nation. And that's why this is such an amazingly difficult moment."

"How are you coping with the grief?" one reporter asked.

"You know, life is full of difficulties, isn't it? We all face it. And I'm just so glad that I know how to handle these things and where I can take my grief. I'm thankful that my belief is that Natasha is in a much better place."

"Does this test your faith?" another asked.

"It absolutely does test my faith in God," I replied. "This is another chink in the armour, and it tests my belief; of course it does. Doubt is a part of faith. Without doubt, you don't have faith. So sure, we're saying to God, 'Why has this happened? Where does this fit into your plan?' And I don't have an answer for that, I'm sorry. But I do have a place to go in my heart and I can trust that we're going to get through this. And not only that, but my other two kids are going to be so much stronger as a result."

Then I remembered something Natasha had said to us just before she left, and it seemed right to share with everyone in closing.

"It was raining when they left. Tash was thinking, 'Oh no, I've got to go down to OPC and do adventure.' She didn't really love adventure, but she'd done enough of it. And I was always proud of her that she would take these things on. And when we said to her, 'Honey, how do you feel about the rain?' She said, 'Oh, my good friend Portia,' (who was in the group and died also), 'and I have this little saying: we're going to jump in puddles.' And she said, 'What I mean by that is even if it's bad, we're going to make the most of it.' And that's what my daughter and Portia were like: 'We're going to jump in puddles.' And I guess that's what all the parents are trying to do now. We're going to try and jump in puddles."

By then, I was ready to just be with Nikki and away from all the people and media.

The next few days were a journey that I wouldn't wish on anyone, although the level of support from around the world was unfathomable. The number of bouquets that arrived by courier meant flowers flowed out the door onto the driveway. Cards, gift baskets, and food poured through our front door as the available room in our house got smaller and smaller.

But in the midst of all of that, we took part in live interviews, made arrangements for an autopsy on Natasha's beautiful body, worked with the undertaker to choose caskets and make funeral arrangements, and continued going through the motions of life with aching hearts. My own heart was breaking, but I had to try to stay strong for Nikki, Olivia, and Ben.

Nikki and I were inseparable immediately after the tragedy—always holding hands and talking to each other tenderly. But because we grieved in separate ways, we had to guard against the onset of isolation. Nikki wanted to talk about Natasha in every conversation, whereas I wanted to withdraw and grieve quietly. Grief makes it difficult to serve your spouse. But I was thankful we'd invested in our marriage over the years to be able to get through this difficult time together. I don't know how we could have coped otherwise. Another "treasure in the darkness".

Nikki and I recalled an afternoon several months earlier when we had stood on our patio sipping coffee and talking about the good things in our life—namely, our family.

"Imagine if we ever lost Natasha," I had said. "Life would be unbearable."

Nikki had agreed. "We wouldn't be able to cope."

Yet we found ourselves having to live with the unbearable. The question that kept coming to my mind as I went through the many stages of grief was, "Why?" I didn't hold God responsible for what happened, but He certainly is powerful enough that He could have saved them. I had to let that go—I couldn't possibly see His plan or understand His perspective on this. I just knew He was grieving alongside us and sustaining us.

Dennis Rainey told me, "Save the 'why' question and ask it of the only person who can truly answer it—Jesus. And when you do, the answer will amaze you."

When I told this to a close friend, his reply was, "And when you hear the answer, our only response will be, 'of course!' "

I also had to deal with my initial anger at OPC for their lack of compliance to safety procedures. What a price to pay for human error! The director gave an apology on TV to all of the parents, which helped. But I eventually had to make the decision to forgive rather than allow anger and bitterness to grow in my heart. God has helped me through this process, and I don't feel any anger now. The other parents also forgave freely and behaved so kindly—truly a testimony to the power of God and His peace and comfort at work.

Even the secular media noticed our community's lack of bitterness and our quiet strength. Our faith truly made all the difference in our response to the tragedy and our ability to cope with it. One TV journalist, a professed non-believer, said on live radio, "Whatever it is they're drinking, I want a sip of it."

We will always miss Natasha terribly. But God promised in His Word to bind up the brokenhearted. Well, we are more broken than we've ever been. But God is working in our hearts and healing us, day by day.

Sometimes it feels as if Nikki and I will never be truly happy again. But we know that's not what Natasha would have wanted. She would have wanted us to go on in joy and to love God and each other more through all of this. She would have wanted those affected by the tragedy, especially non-believers, to turn to God for strength and find what they've been missing. She would have wanted us to look forward to the day when we would be reunited with her in heaven, and in the meantime to "jump in puddles"—her unique way of telling us to find treasures in the darkness.

chapter eleven

leaving a legacy

We often told Natasha that God was going to use her in mighty ways to impact the world and make a difference. It turns out we were right, but in a way much different from what we had envisioned.

Immediately after the accident, it hurt to hear people talking about Natasha's legacy touching the nation—it was far too high a price for us to pay. But over time, it brought us great joy to read the hundreds of letters that poured in from people who had been touched in some way by her life and death.

Some were inspired by her example to write tributes and letters to loved ones, to hug frequently, and to be encouraging. Others were impressed that she had never dated or kissed a boy and made similar pacts of purity. But most noticeable in her life was her love for Jesus.

The world stopped for a while and got a glimpse of how awesome a child of God can be, and many individuals wrote to tell us they had been inspired to live for God by what they'd seen in her life.

Of course, our own family was deeply touched by her legacy as well. We've never taken each other for granted—quite the opposite, as my illness has made us all realize just how precious and short our time on earth together is. But it has caused us to come to a fork in the road where we can either become better people through this or not.

Zig Zigler, who lost his adult daughter, Susan, wrote in *Confessions of a Grieving Christian*, "Above all, we are to maintain a softness of heart and turn to the Lord, rather than become hardhearted and turn away from God." I want to have a soft heart. I want to grow through this.

Natasha has left us a tremendous example of what it means to leave a godly legacy. I began thinking about my own legacy a few years after my stroke, but some time before Natasha's death, when Nikki threw an amazing surprise fiftieth birthday party for me.

"I know you've had some rough times in the last few years," Nikki explained to me as I surveyed dozens of friends who had joined to celebrate with us in a hotel conference room. "I wanted to surprise you with this to show you what you mean to all of us."

Boy, was I surprised! Nikki had asked friends and family to write tributes for my birthday. As I read each one and heard beautiful speeches from her, each of my children, and a few close friends and family members, it struck me that I felt as though I were listening in on my own funeral.

"I wanted you to hear all of these things while you're still with us," Nikki said, not to be morbid, but realistically acknowledging my chances of survival.

I was so touched and humbled by the wonderful things people said. Nikki had arranged for various people to send tributes from the States via video, including Dennis and Barbara Rainey, our mentors Bob and Kathy Helvey, and Bob and Jan Horner. Different people stood up and told us of how their lives had changed through FamilyLife. Nikki wrote me a beautiful letter reminiscing on all the things we had accomplished together, and my children expressed their love and thankfulness to me in creative ways (including a poem from Natasha, a PowerPoint slideshow from Olivia, and a presentation from Ben on how I was like Mr Incredible from the Disney movie *The Incredibles*).

On one hand, I feel very ordinary—almost a bit pathetic due to my illness. I don't feel that my life has been unusually special or that the things I've done have been particularly noteworthy. I've just tried to make the most of my time and the opportunities presented to me, and kept putting one foot in front of the other. At the same time, I don't feel at all that my life has been wasted.

We're all entrusted with a certain amount of time, and we all leave a legacy. The question is, What kind of legacy are we leaving? Have I set a good example of marriage for my children? Has my life reflected the love of Jesus to others? I'm so proud of Natasha and the legacy she has left. She's an example to me of what a godly legacy can be. I was so in awe of her faith, I longed to see what it would look like as she grew up.

I don't worry much about what I'm leaving behind in the world, although that is a part of legacy. God has done amazing things through FamilyLife, and I know He'll continue to take care of it; He'll raise up someone new to keep the ministry going in New Zealand after I'm gone. I've seen glimpses of that each time I've been taken out of the picture for a while, through my stroke and Natasha's death. People have been terrific to step in and keep things going. But I'm more interested in what I'm leaving behind in my children. (Even the primary motivation in writing this book was to pass on my story to them.)

I've seen so many fathers who are working their lives away. There are even people in ministry who are sometimes tempted to sacrifice their marriage or family lives on the altar of a successful ministry, but they forget that one of the best ways we can reach out to the world is by modelling a godly family and by preparing our children to carry on the task of living Christ-like lives after we're gone.

I once heard Dennis Rainey say, "Our children are messengers that we send to a time and a world we will not see." I see future generations ahead of us that really need to know about God. So, it's Nikki's and my responsibility now to make sure our children are equipped with the biblical principles they'll need throughout their lives. Hopefully my children will have learnt a few things like patience, contentment, dependency on God, and the importance of perseverance from my experiences. I pray they don't have to go through the fire for these truths to be sealed to their hearts, but God knows better than I do what they need. And in fact, Ben and Olivia have already had to go through the fire in dealing with their sister's death. I pray God will use that to make them stronger and develop their character.

Psalm 127 says that children are "like arrows in the hands of a warrior." Our ultimate goal as parents is that when we fire these arrows, our children will go into the world with a passion for God and a desire to make a difference. Passing on faith can be a hard thing to do, though. How do you make your children grasp the love of God? Ultimately, we have to leave it in God's hands, but there is still plenty we can do before we launch our arrows to help build character and faith in them.

For a while, I was involved in a men's group that met once a week for a Bible study and accountability. It was good, but with dialysis my free time was very limited. I decided it was more important that I invest my time in building our children's faith, so I pulled out of the men's group and began spending time with each of the children one on one. Each Tuesday morning, I took one of them out for a breakfast at McDonald's to do a Bible study. I didn't want to get caught in the trap of filling my life too full of "good things" that I would miss out on addressing the most pressing needs. I didn't know then how limited my time with Natasha would be, and I still don't know how much longer I'll have with Ben and Olivia. How thankful I am for these special one-on-one times I've spent with them! Nobody, at the end of his life, wishes he had spent more time working, or watching TV, or keeping the house clean.

Making the decision to spend more time with my children reminded me of the jar illustration I use often in a talk we deliver called "Managing Pressure in your Marriage"—you can fill a jar with large rocks and then add pebbles, sand, and water until the jar is completely full. But if you don't put the large rocks in first, you won't have room for them at all. Those "large rocks" are the things that are most important—the time we spend with God or with our family. It's easy to let the pebbles and sand— the little things in life—pile up and push the most important things out.

Spending time with Nikki and the children has been one of my highest priorities. I've apologised to my children from time to time because I couldn't throw them in the air or wrestle with them like I used to, but they didn't seem to mind. They've said, "You're still the best dad in the world."

What's made me "the best dad in the world" in their eyes? There are so many things that I can't do with my children that other dads can, and deep down it really hurts. But I think it's most important for all children to grow up in a loving and secure family that teaches them the incredibly rewarding adventure of living for God.

We've seen Natasha's legacy and how the power of God in her life has left a mark on this world, and is continuing to leave a mark as time goes by. Nothing else could bring Nikki and me greater joy as parents.

I hope that I get to live long enough to see the legacy played out in Ben's and Olivia's lives. I have so many dreams for my children—that they will marry a passionate Christian, if marriage is in God's plan for them; that they will be salt and light, making a difference for Christ in whatever they're doing; that people will be attracted to them because of who they are.

They'll undoubtedly go through more tough times, but I'm confident that God will sustain them by bringing them the treasures of love, joy, contentment, peace, and perseverance to get them through their moments of darkness. Perhaps the most important reason that I can be thankful for the hardships I've endured is that my children have learnt numerous lessons by watching Nikki and me cope together and rely on God for strength when we have been weak and in pain. I think all of those moments they witnessed will go a long way in establishing a legacy that will multiply and flourish long after I'm gone.

Nikki and I tell a story at our marriage conferences that goes like this: A young man who had been married for only a few years visited his father one day to talk about how his marriage was falling apart. "We just can't do it anymore, Dad," said the young man. "We're going to get a divorce." Then he added, "I just wish I had a marriage like you and mum."

The father thought to himself and replayed back in his mind all the trials and struggles he and his wife had worked through over the years, the times they even hated each other, the times when they nearly separated. But because they'd hung in there somehow, they'd overcome and were still happily married after twenty-five years together. He turned to his son and said these profound words, "The truth is, son, if you do quit, you'll never have a marriage like me and mum."

Leaving a godly legacy requires perseverance, commitment, and submission to God's will. But when we put those things together, the legacy we leave behind can change the world—starting with our own family.

epilogue

The only real possibility of relief from regular dialysis is a kidney transplant. It is not a magic wand, as it entails its own complications—mainly because of the highly toxic anti-rejection drugs one has to take—but it can provide a high quality of life. It can also considerably lengthen life expectancy. A successful transplant has an average "life span" of ten years, although some have lasted as many as thirty years.

In my case, I have already received two transplants. The first failed in a matter of days. The second lasted ten years. As a result of these previous transplants, my body developed a high level of antibodies that now negatively affect tissue-typing with potential new donors.

In the last nine years, fourteen generous people have offered themselves as live donors. In most cases, the cross-match has been compatible but the antibodies have gotten in the way. The ironic thing is that Natasha had so wanted to offer me her kidney, but I told her she was far too precious to me at her young age for me to even consider it.

Realising that it was unlikely I would ever get a kidney transplant in the usual course of events, I went searching on the Internet for possible solutions. I soon discovered that at the private Mayo Clinic in Rochester, Minnesota, USA, a successful treatment had been found for a person with the same condition. With facts and figures in hand, Nikki and I arranged a meeting with the head of transplants in New Zealand, Dr Ian Dittmer, and asked him if this treatment was available in New Zealand.

Dr Dittmer was familiar with the treatment but advised that, because of protocols, I was deemed a low priority for a transplant because of my age, previous medical history (cancer, stroke, etc.) and lack of finances. As a result, they were unable to offer this treatment. However, he said they would be willing to endorse such a treatment, even to facilitate things to make it happen, if the money was provided. How much money? $250,000!

With that news, we left the hospital with our tails between our legs. A quarter of a million dollars was just too much money. Even so, we wrote a brief synopsis in a newsletter that went out to a private group of key supporters. David and Joan Cooper received their copy of the newsletter and immediately felt that the money was no real object at all, and after conferring with me, they immediately set about establishing a legal fundraising trust.

Within four months, all the money came in from around the globe in an amazing response, which flabbergasted all of us involved. There had been visions of sausage sizzles, car washes, and selling chocolate bars door-to-door, but none of that proved necessary.

The first to offer money was six-year-old Bjorn Byrne. He was visiting our family and saw his Uncle Andy on the machine. "Why do you need to do that?" Bjorn asked. I briefly explained how the machine kept me alive.

When his mother picked him up a short time later, he told her about the machine. His mother then told him about the idea to raise money for a transplant that would get me off the machine.

"Take me to the bank now, Mum," he said. "I want to give him $51 from my bank account." (He had $56 in his account.) Bjorn withdrew the money and designed a beautiful card shaped like a yacht so Uncle Andy could sail to America and get his new kidney!

Some boys at my son's school spent their weekends washing cars, but most of those who contributed were couples whom we didn't even know. They had attended a FamilyLife Marriage Conference and had their lives and marriages so enhanced that their financial donation was an expression of their gratitude.

If you were given a copy of this book, it's very likely that you were one of those many generous contributors. Thank you for creating this opportunity that may give me and my family a release from the burden of dialysis and a freedom to pursue our ministry to families for many more years to come.

It is now a waiting game as potential new live donors are tested for compatibility. Although we don't yet know the results of this huge effort, we'd like to acknowledge David and Joan Cooper and the other trustees who made the fundraising possible: John and Karen Fitness, Deana Watson, Lyn Birkhead, Malcolm and Biffy Savage, Steve Hooper, and David Munn.

With the death of Natasha still so poignant and painful to bear (I doubt the ache of her loss will ever pass), I have experienced two opposite emotions to the transplant drama. One: What's the point? Why worry? I'd rather go quickly and be with her in paradise; and two: Nikki, Olivia, and Ben need me to live longer more than ever. My sudden demise in the midst of this recent tragedy would be too tough for any of them. It's more important than ever that I stay strong for them. And it is this second emotion that I'm responding to now, by building up my strength and stamina so that if and when a transplant occurs, I'll be at my best to receive and sustain it.

—Andy Bray